P9-DHL-291

# CONTENTS

# CHAPTER 1

# Genesis

*Left:* Michael Jordan finally realized his dream: NBA Champion. He said, "It was a lot of hard work, and what you see is the emotions of all that hard work paying off. Not just for me but for this team and this city. It was a seven-year struggle."

# CHAPTER 1

APPROPRIATELY, this telltale incident took place just outside the Genesis Convention Center in Gary, Indiana, for it would mark the beginning of a legend.

It's not so much how this burgeoning superstar performed on that day in 1984, but rather the powerful impact he had on peoples' lives even before his rookie season began. When Michael Jordan came strolling out, he was totally unprepared for the kind of adoring public that shrieked in worship at the Beatles and Elvis Presley. Hundreds of teenage girls surrounded him, looking to tear away a piece of their idol. Security guards finally led Michael to a waiting automobile, yet once inside, the car wouldn't

Michael drives around the legendary Julius "Dr. J" Erving, in most people's minds the forerunner to Air Jordan.

# GENESIS

budge. Outside, an elderly lady was lying down in front of the car, refusing to move.

"I never got a chance to get his autograph," the lady said.

"If you don't move, the car will run you over," said a security guard.

"That's all right," she replied, "as long as Michael Jordan is in the car."

When word reached Jordan of this touchy predicament, he quickly signed an autograph for the lady and flashed a surprised yet winsome Jordan smile.

"Everywhere we go, it's like he's Michael and we're the Jacksons," said then-teammate Orlando Woolridge in comparing athlete to singer. As Jordan's stardom reached new heights, he pulled along his teammates, an entire franchise, and practically the city of Chicago with him. This is a bustling sports town, the city of broad shoulders, that previously had embraced such superstars as Ernie Banks, Walter Payton, Gale Sayers, Bobby Hull, and Luke Appling. Yet never before had it experienced anything like Michael Jordan.

Jordan may be the first black athlete in America truly to transcend the racial barriers that are slow to crumble. He is an African-American who is portrayed as an all-American guy, a role model for all children. There also exists within Jordan the business acumen and insight to impress the staunchest, most critical heads of multimillion-dollar corporations. It's no wonder the juggernauts of America's free enterprise system—McDonald's, Coca-Cola, Wheaties, Nike, Chevrolet—scramble to

# CHAPTER 1

get his endorsement with million-dollar contracts.

Yet, as easily as Jordan maintains his role as entrepreneur supreme among the three-piece corporate set, he can slip back, more comfortable than ever, into the Peter Pan identity that charms kids of all ages with the magic of the Pied Piper of Hamlin. A caller to a radio talk show recently said, "I wish a sportswriter would print Jordan's anti-drug stance. My two children absolutely adore Michael Jordan and worship the ground he walks on. Once they read what he believes, I wouldn't have to worry about them ever using drugs for the rest of their lives."

Poet e.e. cummings once wrote: "Childhood is the truest vision of the world," and perhaps it is the children, yet untainted by the facades and pretensions of adulthood, that can truly perceive the essence of Michael. What they see is the spirit of a playful little boy, at times unworldly and full of wonderment, still pulsating inside the body of perhaps the world's greatest athlete.

How else could you explain the extraordinary friendship Jordan struck up with a Massachusetts youngster named Josh, who snuck down to the court during North Carolina's NCAA Tournament victory over Georgetown and wound up sitting in Michael's lap afterwards? They became pen pals, long-distance confidants—and while countless sportswriters, TV sportscasters, agents, and others would try desperately to monopolize a few precious minutes of Jordan's time, Josh would call collect and talk for what seemed like hours. A 12-year-old boy had the

# GENESIS

home phone number of one of America's greatest celebrities.

"We admire him for going from a regular black kid to making it in the pros," said Florida teenager Joyce Okamoto. "Kids idolize him. He is kind of like Prince, the rock star, but I don't think anybody compares to Michael Jordan as far as popularity. You hear all the bad things about kids coming out of college and getting into drugs after they make the pros. Michael Jordan is clean, and that's another big reason why we like him. He's not like a rock star, getting big-headed, conceited and flaunting things. He sews his own clothes, cleans house, and does things for himself. He's like a normal person walking around. He doesn't let success go to his head."

What fascinates kids and grownups alike is the sheer magnitude of Jordan's athleticism. Perhaps the single most intriguing characteristic of "Air" Jordan is his ability to defy gravity. He has given a whole new meaning to the term "hang time." He is taking the game of basketball to new heights and awakening a fantasy in all the wish to fly.

"Fly? I don't know," Jordan said. "But when I do, I'll let you know. I'm getting close. I remember one game in Milwaukee, got it on tape, where it looks like I'm taking off. I stole the ball, and I'm rising up. Then, I just stop in midair and start my descent. I shot the ball coming down."

Jordan's first coach with the Bulls, Kevin Loughery, will never forget one night in the 1984-85 season when Jordan appeared to be walking on air. "We were playing the Bullets in Washington,"

# CHAPTER 1

Loughery said, "and you got to understand, Michael's first year we had him, Orlando Woolridge, and not much else. Anyway, Michael's driving towards the circle and begins taking off at the top of key [about 20 feet from the basket]. He looks to his left and spots Ennis Whatley open, except Ennis couldn't hit a jump shot that night to save his life. So, [Michael] glances to his right and there's Wes Matthews, who isn't shooting much better than Ennis. Still in the air, Michael takes one last look back at Ennis then double pumps and banks it in. That's the most amazing thing I've ever seen."

Loughery was witness to one more Jordan fable, this one of the coach's own doing. Loughery had coached "Dr. J," the legendary Julius Erving, in most people's minds the forerunner to Air Jordan. Loughery knew if the young North Carolina rookie wasn't challenged, an immense potential could go to waste.

One day at practice, Loughery tested Jordan. After two and one-half hours of running and jumping and sweating, the coach always had a final scrimmage with the losing team being forced to run an additional 15 laps. Jordan has a passionate hatred of losing, never mind the extra running. It was red jerseys against the white jerseys, first team to score 11 baskets wins. Loughery stacked his five best players against Jordan to no avail. Jordan's red team was winning 7-2 when the coach blew his whistle.

"Michael, switch over to the whites, Rod Higgins, you're on the reds." First came Jordan's incredulous look of disbelief soon followed by one of

10

anger and hurt as Loughery repeated his order. There are two things you don't mess with when it comes to Jordan: his pocketbook and his sense of fair play. He sulked, he pouted, and he ranted at Loughery. He considered walking off the court in protest to this unfair edict.

Finally, he switched jerseys and a look came into his eye that struck a little fear into everyone else on the court. For the next 20 minutes, he was a man possessed, driven by a focus and a concentration few can ever hope to attain. He was at war with the world, and Kevin Loughery had momentarily become Jordan's worst enemy. Jordan called for the ball the first four times and angrily transformed those possessions into two swishes from 18 feet and two electrifying monster dunks, as Jordan seemed to swoop in from somewhere near the ceiling.

Jordan's teammates became tentative, as if they were in the middle of a mystical experience. Maybe they were, for on this November afternoon, they had encountered a force beyond their control. He was everywhere, stealing passes and blocking shots, a one-man basketball terrorist. He continued driving to the hoop and making moves that defy the laws of physics. Scoring seven of the last nine baskets, Jordan led his team to an 11-9 comeback win. The game-winner was a resounding dunk, no doubt Jordan transposing an image of Loughery's face on the cylinder as he slammed the ball through. He walked over to the coach and affixed a mean stare as if to say: "Take that." Loughery just smiled.

From such a colorful beginning, Jordan has

# CHAPTER 1

evolved into the National Basketball Association's premier player, the marquee attraction, the standard by which all other stars are judged. He has led the Bulls to their best season in franchise history. And then, Michael went on to lead his Jordanaires to the NBA promised land.

"My role has changed this season," said Jordan recently. "I've accepted becoming the leader of the team. That meant making sacrifices, not scoring as many points as I had in the past, not taking as many shots. But as long as we're winning, that's all that really counts. I never felt comfortable exerting my leadership capabilities when I first got here. There were too many other veteran players, and why should they listen to me? But I'm one of the older guys now, and the younger players look up to me somewhat for leadership."

Jordan has his share of critics, those who tout the Boston Celtics' Larry Bird and the Los Angeles Lakers' Magic Johnson as superior players because they made those around them better players. At one time, it bothered Jordan that Bird and Magic received so much credit when their respective surrounding casts were so far superior to Jordan's. Bird teams with All-Stars Kevin McHale and Robert Parish and at one time also had stars Dennis Johnson and Danny Ainge. Magic, of course, had the legendary Kareem Abdul-Jabbar plus talents like All-Star James Worthy, Byron Scott, Michael Cooper, and A.C. Green. Jordan had Ennis Whatley and Wes Matthews. Now, the Bulls have increased their talent base, with Scottie Pippen, Horace Grant,

# GENESIS

Bill Cartwright, John Paxson, and B.J. Armstrong.

Chicago is a city that seems cursed with the bridesmaid mentality. Its nickname is "Second City." Whatever Chicago could do, New York would always do better. When the White Sox had their best teams, the Yankees were just a little better. When the Cubs had perhaps their best team ever, they collapsed as the Mets won the 1969 National League pennant. When it came to stage, screen, the arts, business, finance, New York was always looking down at Chicago.

All that changed when an unassuming young rookie from North Carolina came to live in the city of big shoulders. Had Carl Sandburg been around, no doubt he would've set Jordan's heroics to verse. Before Michael first put on No. 23, the Bulls were averaging 6,000 fans a game. Newspaper accounts of the night's proceedings could be found just in front of the obituaries in the metropolitan dailies.

Now, the club continues to set attendance records. It's headed toward 200 consecutive sellouts, and there is a waiting list the length of Manute Bol's arm for season tickets. The Bulls have become the hottest show in town, and Jordan is the conductor.

Kim Adams, a Philadelphia television anchorwoman, recalls her first exposure to Chicago Stadium on West Madison Street. She stared in wonderment as the house lights went down with the flair of a Broadway production and the spotlights began flashing during the introduction of the Bulls' players. When it came time for Jordan to take a bow, the roar of 18,000 fans reached a crescendo.

# CHAPTER 1

"My ears, I've never heard cheering like that before," said Adams, who has taken in Philly's finest ovation for Charles Barkley and was around when Dr. J would make his periodic house calls. "The cheering for Jordan, especially, I was really moved. The enthusiasm of the crowd, the place is filled to the rafters. I'm not used to this, and it's not even the playoffs yet. It's great to be a part of it. Philadelphia fans are very supportive of their teams, too. But I've never witnessed this level of enthusiasm before during the regular season. Is it all because of Michael Jordan?"

A rare chemistry works inside Michael. He has a combination of some incredible genes thrown in with a humble upbringing by parents who made sure his feet were firmly entrenched in terra firma long before he ever took flight. His is the saga of small-town country boy who didn't get swept away in the glamorous, jet-setting, big-money, fast-cars lifestyle that has seduced so many before him. There is something pulsating inside the man that seems to keep his equilibrium balanced. Those who are close to him can sense it, almost feel it, yet it's nearly impossible to describe. Maybe it's the goodness of a soul, the sensitivity within a heart, the common sense simply to be happy with who you are, no matter what.

On Easter Sunday in 1988, Jordan hit his first 20 of 24 shots to score 59 points in a stunning upset of the Detroit Pistons at the Pontiac Silverdome on national TV. He danced around in the locker room afterwards, and even an hour delay at the Detroit airport for the flight home couldn't dampen his spirits.

When the Bulls were finally called to board their first-class seats, Jordan headed to the ramp. On the way, he spotted a young girl leaning on crutches. "Aren't you with us?" he asked, figuring she should be accorded early boarding privileges along with the dozen trim athletes who were receiving special treatment. "I wish I were," she replied. "You are now," Jordan said. He put his arm around the girl and escorted her aboard. "She's with us," Jordan explained to a smiling gate attendant.

There has to be a reason that so many admire Jordan when there are other athletes and entertainers who should be able to generate the same kinds of reactions. To be sure, there is a certain charisma at work here, a flamboyance mixed with a little boy's naïveté. Jordan does things the average man cannot, yet smiles and laughs at it. He doesn't look down at folks in midflight; rather, he encourages "come fly with me." He has no qualms about letting his reality become our fantasy. Those who are gifted often want to hoard their specialness. To Jordan, what would be the fun in that? He would rather share his God-given talents.

About the magnanimous owner of the San Francisco 49ers, Eddie DeBartolo Jr., O.J. Simpson once said that he "spends money the way we all would like to think we would." You might make the same claim for Michael, that he shares his abilities and special gifts the way we all would like to think we would if we were in his Air Jordans.

# CHAPTER 2

# From Brooklyn to Wilmington

*Left:* Jordan, pictured in his high school yearbook, became serious about basketball as a sophomore at Laney High School. He wasn't elevated to varsity as a sophomore because coach Fred Lynch felt Michael needed more height. Instead, 6'7" Leroy Smith took the spot that would have belonged to Michael.

# CHAPTER 2

IT ALL BEGAN on February 17, 1963, when Michael Jordan was born in a Brooklyn, New York, hospital. The fourth child of James and Deloris Jordan didn't exactly come sailing into the world.

Working while five months pregnant and raising three young children gave Deloris many hardships in the fall of 1962. That was when her mother died unexpectedly. Hoping to avoid any possibility of a miscarriage, doctors ordered her to stay in bed for a week. "I always said that Michael's birth was like a sign," Deloris said. "I lost my mother unexpectedly while carrying Michael, and he was my godsend. Michael was the happiness He sent me after a very sad time in my life."

"The near miscarriage was very bad," said James, who had moved the family temporarily from their beloved North Carolina to New York so he could take vocational classes to expand his income potential. "When Michael was born, we thought there might be something wrong with him. He was born with a nosebleed. The hospital kept him three days after Deloris was discharged. He'd have nosebleeds for no reason until he was 5 years old. Then, they just stopped."

"My nose still bleeds easily," Jordan said. "That's one story my mom never told me. The only thing my mom told me was the time when I fell behind the bed as a baby and almost suffocated. There have been some very close calls in terms of my life."

It couldn't come any closer than the time Jordan

was nearly electrocuted at age 2. James was tuning up the family car in the backyard of his parents' home in Wallace, North Carolina, and the ground was still drenched from an earlier rainstorm. To light the engine, he had extended a couple of wires from the house. Although preoccupied with his work, James still noticed something moving out of the corner of his eye. Michael was intrigued by the extension cord, making it a father-and-son project. James went after Michael, but it was too late. Michael was scrutinizing the juncture of the two live wires. He touched the live wires together and was knocked about three feet back. "I've thought to myself since: 'My God, how this world would've been cheated if the cord had gotten tangled up with Michael and not let him go,'" James said. "He would've been electrocuted."

It's not shocking to learn that Jordan is family-oriented. Just as the Japanese culture puts a premium on the importance of the family, so too did the Jordans raise their five children. The inner-strength that lets Michael climb to amazing heights is rooted in the backyard of the Jordan family home in Wilmington, North Carolina.

Watch Michael carefully, listen to his words. There is the unmistakable presence of an inner discipline. Someone taught him early on the virtues of courtesy, honesty, the respect of elders. Nothing is more important to Jordan than his family. "My family has been my inspiration to succeed," Jordan said. "My childhood means a lot to me. They were pushing me and fighting with me and helping me become the man I am today. My personality and my laughter come from my father. My business and serious side come from my mother."

Deloris said that Michael was leaning toward his father's personality when he was small. "He was such a jolly baby," she said. "He never cried. Just feed him and give him something to play with, and he was fine. He doesn't like sadness. He gets very quiet around that. Once, a girlfriend of his drowned when he was in college. He took it very badly. He wants to make it right, no matter what it is. He doesn't want problems. He wants everybody to be happy."

As most children do, Michael also had his mischievous side. "You had to discipline him," Deloris said. "He would test you to the limit. Michael was always getting into things." For

Michael, pictured in the high school cafeteria, developed into an excellent player by his senior season.

example, when Michael was 12 and brother Larry 13, their father had dug a drainage ditch behind the house and left a tall mound of dirt beside it. This was around the time when motorcycle daredevil Evel Knievel was making headlines, and the Jordan brothers liked to play around on a little motorbike. One day the brothers tried to confront the ultimate test of hang time. They backed up the scooter about 300 yards from the pile of dirt and, with Michael driving and Larry sitting behind, attempted to launch themselves up the mound and over the water. Just as Evel had missed clearing the Snake River, the two boys didn't clear the ditch.

Both were unharmed except for the bruises and scratches they tried to hide from their father that night. They received a painful punishment from their father that evening and proceeded to sell the motorbike the next day.

Jordan thought that he was, in his own words, "goony looking," and so feared no one would want to marry him that he took a home economics course in school. Wanting to fend for himself, he learned how to cook, sew, and clean. "I remember he baked a cake in school that was so good we couldn't believe it," Deloris said. "We had to call his teacher to verify it."

"Michael is probably the laziest kid I had," said James, who grew up the son of a poor farmer and was driving a tractor by the age of 10. "If he had to get a job in a factory punching a clock, he'd starve to death. He would give every last dime of his allowance to his brothers and sisters and even kids in

Jordan averaged 23 points a game as a senior and was named
to the Mid-Eastern All-Conference Team and the
McDonald's All-American Team.

the neighborhood to do his chores. He was always broke."

Michael was always a popular kid, and he learned early the lessons in racial equality passed down to him from his father. James's family had a close relationship with a white family, the Teachers. Times were tough, and folks in the community banded together. When the Teachers had a newborn child but the mother couldn't spare time to nurse him, James's mom nursed the baby. When the Jordan family welcomed a new member, the Teachers would return the favor. The Jordan and Teacher kids grew up as almost family during an intolerant time.

Michael's father and mother met when James was age 18 and living in Wallace, some 30 miles from Deloris, age 15, who lived in Rocky Point, North Carolina. It wasn't exactly love at first sight. If not for James's persistence, there might never have been a Michael Jordan as we know him.

"A bunch of us were riding home from school one day, and when James came to let me out of the car, he said: 'Oh, I didn't know you were in the car. You're cute. Someday, I'm going to marry you.' From then on, I thought he was a little fresh. I stayed away from him," Deloris remembered. "He kept after me. Eventually, I went out with him and saw the other side. What attracted me was his personality. As far as looks, it was no more than some of the other guys. He was outgoing, had a good sense of humor and was very concerned, a kind person. We became friends before anything else.

# CHAPTER 2

Once we began dating seriously, my parents thought
it was too intense. So, they sent me off to Tuskegee
Institute in Alabama for college. He went into the
Air Force. During one break from school, I went
home and he was there on a leave. I never went
back to college." Although James was transferred to
a base in Virginia, he continued the courtship. After
proposing in April of 1957, James and Deloris
Jordan were married in September.

"I grew up on a farm without the luxuries a lot
of kids have," James said. "I came from a small
farming town. If one family owned a television, the
other 10 families would come over to watch it.
There were farm chores, and when I was 17, I drove
a school bus part-time. By 7:30 p.m., I'd be back at
school playing ball. I was a pretty good player, but
never had the height. At least half of our high school
games were played on outdoor courts because our
school couldn't afford an indoor gym. In junior
high, I had a cousin who was 6'11" and there were a
couple other kids 6'10". Black schools only played
black schools and never got any exposure like kids
get now. Segregation was very prominent in the
South. Restaurants had black and white entrances,
and black people usually entered through the
kitchen.

"I grew up in a neighborhood where everybody
was poor, black and white. We were forced to share
by nature. Mathis and Ann Teacher were our closest
neighbors. We all worked in the fields together,
black and white. I was fortunate I grew up in such
an environment."

# FROM BROOKLYN TO WILMINGTON

Somehow, James the father has been able to impart to his son Michael the humble beginnings and a feeling of being grateful for what you have. Listen closely to the father, and remember when you hear it from the son.

"Deloris and I grew up among whites and got along," James said. "It's not really what color you are, it's who you are. It's not what you amass or have that makes you different, it's your personality. You can have the most money in the world and still be a jerk. You can have no money at all and be the nicest man in the world. People like you for what you are, those are your real friends. We made sure they understood that lesson. None of my kids were ever touched by segregation."

"That's the greatest lesson I've learned from my parents," Michael said. "I never see you for the color. I see you for the person you are. I know I'm recognized as being black, but I don't look at you as black or white, just as a person. I think one of the reasons I've been accepted by people of so many different races is that my personality fits that. I grew up with David Bridges, who is white, since we were 5 years old, and we're still very close. I roomed with Buzz Peterson [who is white] in college." Perhaps Jordan's closest black friend is Adolph Shiver, whom Michael befriended at the age of 12.

Michael is more comfortable and trusting with those who knew and liked him from before than the Johnny-come-latelies who are clutching onto a piece of him in his ever-ascending stardom. One of his best friends is George Koehler, who started to drive

# CHAPTER 2

Michael's limo after Jordan moved to Chicago. They practically lived together before Jordan got married. When it became impractical for Michael to stop in and purchase one of his culinary favorites, Kentucky Fried Chicken, it was always Koehler who would make the run. Jordan came to rely on him for all the little things in life, and the companionship of a good friend.

Growing up in Wilmington, Michael was closest to his older brother by a year, Larry. The ferocity of their backyard one-on-one games has taken on near-legendary proportions. Talk about blood, sweat, and tears, their confrontations were the epitome of competitiveness. Larry, at 5'8", can outjump the famed Air Jordan. For the longest time, Larry was a better player, usually getting the best of his little brother in these sibling showdowns. "Oh yeah, I used to be able to take him most of the time," said Larry, who competed for one season in the World Basketball League for players 6'4" and under, dunking two-handed, backwards, with ease. "But once he began shooting up and getting taller, I had more trouble staying with him."

"Those backyard games really helped me become the player I am today in a lot of ways," Michael said. "Larry would never give me any slack, never took it easy on me. He'd rather beat me up than have me beat him in a game. I learned a lot about being competitive from him."

That homemade court was often alive with games from dawn 'til dusk. "We'd have every kid in the neighborhood at our house in Wilmington

because it was the only one with a basketball court,"
James said. "There would be 20 guys over between
the ages of 10 and 18. That's how Michael learned
to play. We were almost like a park. Deloris would
buy 15 pounds of hot dogs and hamburgers and
we'd make a picnic out of it. When Michael got
older, he'd have the whole North Carolina team over
to the house. They'd stay over and go to the beach
the next day. They'd be sprawled all over, sleeping
on the couch, the floor, everywhere. But we loved
having them, every last one of them."

James Jordan moved his family of five children
to Wilmington when Michael was age 7, Besides
Larry, there is the oldest son James Ronald, and
sisters Delois and Roslyn, the baby of the family.
Ronald is a career man in the Army, stationed in
New Jersey. Delois Chasten lives in Philadelphia
with her husband and two children. Larry and
Roslyn live in Charlotte and work with their parents
in the "Flight 23 By Jordan" sports stores that sell
Air Jordan apparel.

Mom, dad, Larry, and Roslyn run three Flight
23 By Jordan stores that sell exclusively a complete
line of MJ's sports apparel and Air Jordan shoes.
James and Deloris are in charge of the thriving
business that did more than $2 million worth of sales
last year. Larry is a vice president and oversees one
of the stores, while Roslyn helps her mother.

"We don't keep enough of Michael's products in
stock," said James, who did well during the NBA
All-Star Weekend in Charlotte and expected business
to boom when the NCAA's Final Four comes to

Charlotte next year. James told the *Chicago Tribune,* "four of my kids have done well in life, one has done overly well. He finds it in his heart to share."

"I never want them to feel that they're not a part of my success," Michael said to the *Tribune.* "My parents, brothers and sisters are very prideful people. They like to work for their own things. I have to actually make them accept some things I want them to have. Still, I'm willing to help them in any way possible." Such as the home he had built for his parents in Charlotte.

"Yes, it has opened some doors for me," Larry told the *Tribune* about business contacts made through his job at Flight 23. "I get different kinds of business proposals every day. I'm always meeting people who want to do things even outside of sportswear. I'm still learning, and it's fun to be working with my family."

Basketball wasn't Michael's first love. If he had a choice, he would have been the next Ernie Banks or Hank Aaron. Baseball was his best sport growing up, particularly when he was merely a normal-sized youngster. "My favorite childhood memory, my greatest accomplishment was when I got the Most Valuable Player award when my Babe Ruth League team won the state baseball championship," he said. "That was the first big thing I accomplished in my life, and you always remember the first." Jordan claims to this day that he treasures that baseball championship even more than the NCAA title he helped bring to North Carolina in 1982 with the game-winning shot or the Olympic gold medal he earned with the U.S. squad two years later.

"The way he played baseball in Little League, he made me become a fan," James said. "If I wouldn't take him to play ball, he'd look so pitiful, like he'd lost every friend in the world and was all by himself. You'd take one look at him and say, 'OK, let's go.' He would do things in baseball and excel beyond kids his age that you would just get caught up in it."

Michael Jordan, however, wasn't born a basketball phenom. He wasn't some hardwood child prodigy like Isiah Thomas, who was competing with 13-year-olds when he was 7. Perhaps Jordan's late blossoming contributes to the modesty and humility he displays today. He became serious about the sport as a sophomore at Laney High School, averaging 25 points a game as the star of the junior varsity. He fully expected a promotion that season to the big time where he would become the next darling of Carolina.

It never happened. Instead, he was cut from the varsity squad and had to resign himself with junior varsity competition. He worked on his game that summer in relentless fashion to make certain he never again suffered such a fate. Over and over he practiced moves that would one day become part of his seemingly limitless repertoire. Even his beloved baseball had to take a backseat to this determination to prove to the Laney coach and everyone else that a mistake had been made the previous season.

Jordan wasn't elevated to the Laney High

varsity team as a sophomore primarily because coach
Fred Lynch felt Michael needed more height.
Instead, the 6'7" Leroy Smith took the spot that
would have belonged to Michael. That made Jordan
work that much harder in the offseason following his
sophomore year. As a junior, Jordan not only made
Lynch's club, but Michael worked his way into the
starting lineup by averaging 20 points a game.

"He could do more things than the average high
school player," recalled Ruby Sutton, Laney's
volleyball and boy's tennis coach. "Still, he was a
normal student. Because he was good at what he did,
that didn't make him a conceited person. And yes,
he stuck his tongue out even back then."

His junior season, he made the varsity team and
went on to have a fair career. Jordan's game began
to come together as a senior, averaging 23 points a
game. Although he was named to the Mid-Eastern
All-Conference Team and the McDonald's All-
American Team, college recruiters weren't exactly
staking out the Jordan home trying to sign him to a
national letter of intent. Teachers and administrators
at Laney even urged him to enroll at a service
academy or at least set his sights realistically—like
attending a small Division III college where he
would get a chance to play.

Jordan said he will never forget the treatment he
received during his senior season. There was one
postseason all-star game in particular when he was
riding the same bus with future Maryland star, the
highly recruited Adrian Branch. This smooth 6'6"
forward was one of the nation's most sought-after

players, the kind who would attract dozens of college scouts. Back then, Jordan was a nobody. Jordan remembers how cocky Branch acted towards him, as if this unknown kid from a small town didn't belong on the same bus. In 1985, the Bulls drafted Branch out of Maryland. Jordan, a seasoned second-year pro, went at Branch hard during preseason training camp. Now, their roles had been reversed. Branch was the untested, hesitant rookie going against the NBA's reigning Rookie of the Year. Jordan's eyes would light up whenever coach Stan Albeck assigned Branch to guard him. It was no contest as Jordan carved this poor rookie up, perhaps in repayment for the treatment Jordan suffered five years earlier.

James looks back on how he raised Michael, smiles and shakes his head.

"There is a message you can tell parents, not that we didn't mess up at times," he said. "In as much as Michael learned a lot growing up, Deloris and I learned a lot as he grew up. All that has happened, I had no idea. Maybe it's better. If I had, I might've pushed him too hard and screwed him up. As it was, everything happened very naturally. Here's a kid who grew up with nothing and always had to work to make ends meet. He came out of a city where they never recruited a player. I look at it, think about it quite often.

"I've got to believe one thing. One day, God was sitting around and decided to make himself the perfect basketball player. He gave him a little hardship early in life to make him appreciate what he would earn in the end, and called him Michael Jordan."

# King of
# Chapel Hill

*Left:* Michael was the consensus College Player of the Year in 1983-84, leading the North Carolina Tar Heels to a 27-2 regular-season record. He averaged 19.6 points per game and 5.3 rebounds per game that season.

# CHAPTER 3

**T**HERE ARE ANY NUMBER of glorious moments in the tradition-steeped legacy of North Carolina University basketball. If you ask any Tar Heel fan or probably most college basketball fans in the state for the most memorable event, though, they'll tell you all about the NCAA championship game in 1982 when a freshman

stepped up and hit the game-winning shot.

That was no ordinary freshman, of course. Yet, even though that first-year Tar Heel was Michael Jordan, we're still talking about some kid who had just turned 19 years old making a shot that had immense ramifications on the entire North Carolina program.

North Carolina coach Dean Smith, the wise, overseeing mentor of the family in Chapel Hill, North Carolina, had been to the Final Four before but had problems coming home on top. In 1977, it was widely acknowledged that Carolina had the best team in the country. Unfortunately, injuries to Phil Ford, Tom LaGarde, and Walter Davis left them subpar and unable to beat Marquette and Al McGuire for the title. In 1981, once again the college basketball consensus was the best unit resided in Chapel Hill. This time, the Tar Heels lost to Indiana.

Had Jordan missed perhaps the biggest shot of his career, Smith would've missed again. Imagine what his detractors would have said when in 1984, Jordan's junior year, the Tar Heels again had the No. 1 team and lost to a nondescript Indiana ballclub in the regional semifinals.

Folks would be wondering if maybe Dean Smith, as great a coach as he is, just doesn't have what it takes to win it all.

It never came to that, thanks to Jordan. The late-bloomer out of Laney High School in Wilmington, North Carolina, wasn't in such demand. He went to UNC because of his admiration and

# CHAPTER 3

respect for Smith. "You'll never play there," friends and advisers told him. "At least you'll have a good seat for every game," they teased. The Michael Jordan we know today was already beginning to emerge. He played 34 games that first year, averaging 13.5 points and 4.4 rebounds while shooting 53.4 percent. At the time, he was one of only eight freshmen ever to start for Smith, who favors the gradual development of his recruits. Jordan was good enough to be named the Atlantic Coast Conference's Freshman of the Year, no small accomplishment in what often is considered the best college basketball league in the land.

So it was, unbeknownst to Jordan, Smith's reputation on the line in the final game of the tournament. Georgetown, with the fearsome 7' Patrick Ewing and the slithering Eric "Sleepy" Floyd led 62-61 with 31 seconds left when Smith signaled he wanted a timeout. "It's very unusual for coach Smith to want a timeout in a situation like that," said North Carolina sports information director Rick Brewer, who's been documenting Tar Heel lore for 20 years. "Coach Smith believes his players are so well schooled, let them run a play and don't give the other team a chance to set up a defense."

Smith sat his five starters down—Jordan, James Worthy, Sam Perkins, Jimmy Black, Matt Doherty—and mapped out his strategy. The first option was to work the ball inside to either the future L.A. Laker all-pro Worthy, who would finish with 28 points, or Perkins, now reunited with

Worthy in Hollywood. That made sense because going inside, if you don't get the two points, you often draw a foul.

Somehow, the venerable Smith had a sense something else was about to unfold, which is why he is considered one of the best college coaches of all time. His sixth sense told him neither Worthy nor Perkins would have the hero's mantle thrust upon them. No, if it was to happen, if this Final Four bugaboo was to be eradicated, it would be by the freshman Jordan. Maybe deep down, Dean even knew that it would be a harbinger of things to come.

So as the Tar Heels broke their huddle and headed back to the court, Smith turned to Jordan and said: "Do it Michael, just knock it in." Sure enough, Ewing menacingly closed down the inside, discouraging the Carolina passers from executing their prime directive. The Tar Heels eventually swung it back around to Jordan. The moment is captured on film, forever being replayed during "March Madness." It is one of the most famous shots in the history of the game. He is 16 feet away from the basket on the left wing and there's 15 seconds showing on the clock. Up he goes, unleashing that patented jumper that would become deadly in the NBA.

Michael's father, James, covered his face, afraid to watch what destiny had in store for his fourth child. How did he know what happened? Was it from the crowd's reaction? "I knew from Deloris [Michael's mother]," James said. "She said something you can't repeat. She screamed: 'Holy (barnyard expletive), he made it!'"

It was the shot by which all other game-winners would be measured. When Michael missed the last-second jumper that could have beaten the Celtics in overtime during the 1986 playoffs, teammate Sidney Green said he figured it was going in because it was just like the Georgetown shot. Even Jordan's most dramatic moment as a pro, the last-second 16-footer that eliminated Cleveland in the first round of the 1989 playoffs, wasn't quite as significant. The Cavaliers shot did bury a once-promising contender, but the Georgetown shot earned a national championship.

"That shot didn't change him that much," Brewer said. "He was a vastly improved player his sophomore year, but most coaches believe that's when a player makes his biggest stride. Maybe that shot did give him a little boost, a little more confidence. A lot of people claim he really didn't know what he was doing when he took that shot."

Maybe he didn't realize it at the time, but what occurred was the baptism of what has become a living legend. He went on a European tour that summer, his first basketball experience abroad. He returned to Chapel Hill and began dominating the game.

The Tar Heels didn't start out the next season like defending champions. They dropped their first two games on the road to St. John's and Missouri. Tulane came into Carmichael Arena ready to extend North Carolina's losing streak. The last time UNC had lost the first three games was 1929. If it happened again, there would've been depression throughout the state. A pair of Tulane free throws provided the visitors with a 53-51 lead with only eight seconds left. Jordan was whistled for an offensive foul with four seconds to go. Tulane took the ball out underneath the Tar Heels' basket. Jordan stole the inbounds pass, turned and hit a 35-footer just before the buzzer. Today, it would've won the game as a three-pointer. Back then, it meant overtime. North Carolina would need three extra sessions before finally subduing Tulane 70-68.

On February 10, 1983, at Carmichael Arena, No. 1-ranked Virginia Cavaliers and 7'4" Ralph Sampson were the victims of Jordan's next miracle in what Brewer described as his most memorable regular-season game during the Jordan era. The Cavs had built a 16-point lead with 8:43 to play, and with 4:00 left, the Tar Heels had come within 10 points. With the Chicago Bulls, the final minutes of a game came to be known as "Jordan Time." On this day, UNC battled back and was trailing 63-60 when Jordan soared over Sampson and tipped in a shot with 1:04 to go. Then, with 52 seconds left, Jordan stole the ball and went the length of the court for a dunk. Carolina protected that lead and when Virginia missed its final shot, it was Jordan wrestling the crucial rebound away from Sampson in the 64-63 win.

Perhaps Michael's best defensive play while at Chapel Hill came at the expense of Maryland and wily coach Lefty Driesell. North Carolina was protecting a one-point lead in Jordan's sophomore

season when Maryland called timeout. The crafty
Driesell inserted seldom-used benchwarmer Chuckie
Driesell, his son, into the game, gambling that the
Tar Heels would pay little heed. He was right.
When play resumed, Chuckie snuck away from his
man, got the ball and headed in for what appeared
to be an uncontested layup. Jordan had been
guarding one of Maryland's top players out near the
top of the circle when he saw Driesell heading in for
the winning basket. He took two long strides then
took off, pinning Driesell's shot cleanly against the
backboard and saving the game.

"Lefty looked like he just about died," said
*Charlotte Observer* sportswriter Leonard Laye, who
covered that game.

Jordan went on to average 20 points, grab five
and one-half rebounds, and shoot 53.5 percent in his
second season, averaging close to two steals a game.
He averaged 19.6 a game after his junior season,
good enough to lead the ACC, with 5.3 rebounds a
game while shooting 55.1 percent. His career high in
college was 39 points against Georgia Tech as a
sophomore.

His final year at Chapel Hill before skipping his
senior season for the pros, Jordan played on a
Carolina team that was considered the best college
team in the country. There were four future NBA
stars on that squad—Jordan, Perkins, point guard
Kenny Smith (Houston Rockets), and center Brad
Daugherty (Cleveland Cavaliers). It was a huge
disappointment when the Tar Heels lost to Indiana
72-68 in the "Sweet 16" at the NCAA tournament.

# KING OF CHAPEL HILL

Early foul trouble for Jordan and Perkins forced
Dean Smith to pull them out, giving the young
Hoosiers a chance to build confidence and believe
they could upset a team that had been ranked No. 1
for most of the season. That final Jordan club would
finish 28-3, including a 14-0 mark in the competitive
ACC.

Nevertheless, the college player of the year
didn't come to the NBA on a down note. Michael
wound up playing for the U.S. on the Olympic
basketball team at the 1984 Summer Games in Los
Angeles. The coach of that team was none other
than the Hoosiers' Bobby Knight, the man who had
sent Jordan home a loser in his college finale.

One of Jordan's favorite stories involves Knight
and the Olympics. "Coach Knight had worked us
real hard and gotten us ready for the Gold Medal
game," Jordan said. "He was a tough coach. You
didn't mess around with him. Anyway, he had
gathered us together and was about to give his
pregame speech when he was called out into the
hallway for something. While he was gone, I went
up to the blackboard and wrote a message for coach:
'You've gotten us ready, and we know what we have
to do.' I was scared. You know how Coach Knight
can be. I wasn't sure what he would do or how he
would react. But I just wanted to let him know that
he had prepared us the best he could, and the rest
was up to us.

"He came back into the room, looked at the
blackboard, looked back at us and said: 'Guess
there's nothing more I can say. Let's go.'" The U.S.

# CHAPTER 3

team, which had blown away all their previous opponents, had little problem winning the Gold. The No. 1 challenger, the Soviet Union, had boycotted that Olympics. It was the last time the U.S. would win the Gold Medal, and Jordan was decidedly the standout throughout the competition.

Members of the press who covered those games still complain about Knight's policy of not featuring one player. Although Jordan was the main man in many games, Knight only brought him to the interview area once. Apparently, the Indiana coach preferred to keep him in the background.

Jordan has since confided to friends that period of training and working out under Knight was the most grueling stretch of basketball he'd ever experienced. "Man, I don't know how you played a whole career for him," Jordan once told Indiana's Steve Alford. Yet, there was a strong mutual respect between the two. To this day, Jordan still opens his eyes wide at the mention of Knight's name. At a celebrity roast honoring Knight, Jordan got up to the rostrum, looked over at the honored guest and said: "Coach Knight is a lot like Coach Smith, except the language is a little different."

Knight will tell you Jordan is the best player he has ever coached. While the '84 Olympic team was playing an exhibition game against a team of NBA players, the U.S. club went seven minutes without Jordan taking a shot. Knight called for a timeout and said: "You've been practicing against Jordan all these weeks, why hasn't he taken a shot? Get him the ball!"

# KING OF CHAPEL HILL

Fulfilling a promise to his parents after he left school a year early, Jordan returned to North Carolina in the summers after his first two NBA seasons to finish his degree in geography. As with all his players, whether they are NBA, MBA, or working construction in some small town, Smith keeps in close contact. The coach and Jordan talk about once a week, without fail. Whenever Jordan has a problem, he'll consult his college coach. (When Perkins signed with the Lakers, Smith was the first person Sam called.)

Jordan is, and always will be, in love with UNC. When the Bulls played a preseason game in Chapel Hill in 1986, before the players stepped off the plane, Jordan announced loudly, "You all be sure to wipe your feet before you get off. You're in God's country now." The first thing he did upon greeting Smith was whisper something in the coach's ear. Smith smiled and told Jordan to follow him. They walked down a long hallway and arrived at a supply room where Smith piled four boxes onto Jordan's waiting arms. The little boy in Jordan took over as he squealed in delight, his eyes big and bright. Inside the boxes were pairs of UNC practice shorts. In his early years in the NBA, Jordan would wear them faithfully, everywhere. Underneath the most expensive tuxedo would be those Carolina blue shorts. "I don't go anywhere without my Carolina blues," he was fond of saying. Now, no matter how rich and famous he becomes, it will always be: "North Carolina's Michael Jordan."

He wouldn't want it any other way.

# CHAPTER 4

# Rare Rookie

*Left:* Michael was drafted third in the 1984, after Akeem Olajuwon and Sam Bowie. All Jordan did was trigger a pro basketball renaissance in Chicago. He came to town highly recommended, yet nobody expected this would be the dawning of perhaps the biggest superstar the sport has even known.

# CHAPTER 4

**Y**OU ALMOST FELT as if the sport of
professional basketball owed this one to
Chicago. No one who swears by the best pizza
in America and ever voted for one of the Richard
Daleys for mayor will ever forget the NBA draft of
1979, at time when Chicago was indeed a second
city. The Bulls had finished with the worst record in
the Eastern Conference, and the Lakers had
shrewdly dealt away journeymen players in exchange
for a coin-toss opportunity at drafting the fabulous
Earvin "Magic" Johnson. This was the prelottery
era, when a simple "heads or tails" determined the
No. 1 pick.

The Lakers won and would make Magic for
another decade. The Bulls lost and wound up with
David Greenwood. So it seemed only fair that five
years later, the Bulls would wind up with Michael
Jordan, courtesy of the Portland Trail Blazers. This
time, Chicago didn't have an opportunity to blow it.
Selecting first, the Houston Rockets grabbed Akeem
Olajuwon. Next came the Blazers, and they opted
for center Sam Bowie. The Bulls were "forced" to
take the North Carolina guard.

All Jordan did was trigger a pro basketball
renaissance in Chicago. He came to town highly
recommended, yet nobody expected this would be
the dawning of perhaps the biggest superstar the
sport has even known. The opener in Chicago
Stadium even made it appear that the $6 million,
seven-year contract might have been a bit too much.
In his NBA debut, a visibly nervous Jordan made
just five of 16 shots to finish with 16 points and

seven assists in a 109-93 victory over Washington before a crowd of 13,913. Believe it or not, at one time there were plenty of tickets available for a Bulls' game and Jordan actually did play like a normal ballplayer.

Not for long. After scoring 21 points the next night in a loss at Milwaukee, Jordan cut loose in only his third game with 37 points in beating the Bucks during a rematch at the Stadium. On a night when the Bulls petulant Quintin Dailey didn't show up for work, Jordan led the way to a 116-110 win by scoring 20 of his team's final 26 points.

"He was sensational," Bucks coach Don Nelson said. "Down the stretch, we couldn't do anything with him. We tried double-teaming him and he just jumped right over it." Milwaukee guard Mike Dunleavy, now the Lakers coach, said, "He showed tremendous poise. Very few rookies can come into the NBA and dominate like this kid."

These were the days when the Bulls were known as "Michael and the Jordanaires." Orlando Woolridge might have been the only other legitimate big-time player. Jordan was surrounded by a cast that included Dave Corzine, Caldwell Jones, Jawann Oldham, Sidney Green, Steve Johnson, Wes Matthews, Ennis Whatley, Rod Higgins, and David Greenwood. Yet, mainly because of the irrepressible rookie, the Bulls jumped out to a 5-2 start, their best in 11 years.

Jordan's first visit to the media mecca of America, New York, created quite a stir. Even though New Yorkers have a well-deserved reputation as a tough, sophisticated crowd, 19,252 fans jammed into Madison Square Garden to witness the latest basketball phenomenon. Late in the Bulls' 121-106 victory, Jordan stole the ball from Darrell Walker, raced upcourt with one glance back at the trivial pursuit, cradled the ball in one hand, shook it twice, and slammed a vicious tomahawk dunk. Posters were made from a photo of that move, it was that dramatic. As one, the sold-out Garden crowd rose up to give Jordan a standing ovation.

The always tough New York press fell all over themselves trying to interview Michael in the post-game locker room. "Michael Jordan, get your own building," Matthews shouted out as the spillover from the media mob at Jordan's locker made it difficult to get dressed.

Jordan answers questions from the Chicago media at a press conference to announce his $6 million, seven-year contract.

# RARE ROOKIE

The Bulls would become accustomed to such treatment. Everywhere they went, there were mobs of reporters, radio and TV broadcasters, and even team officials who would engulf Jordan in a sea of humanity. The young Jordan was fresh, clean-cut, and tremendously accommodating. He would sit patiently, sometimes for as long as an hour afterwards, making sure every query was answered. He would look you straight in the eye, often pausing as he reflected on every answer. It was a luxury the media was unprepared for, since most stars casually rattle off formula responses and then skip out of the locker room as quickly as possible.

Jordan was different. In his junior year at North Carolina, coach Dean Smith had taken him aside and urged him to enroll in a public speaking class. Smith said that Jordan would become an NBA star on his ability alone, yet learning how to deal with the media would only enhance his image. "Is he always like that?" asked a radio broadcaster in Oakland during the Bulls' first West Coast swing. "He is unbelievable. That's one of the best interviews I ever got, and I was one of the last guys to talk to him."

Moments later, an exhausted Jordan walked onto a hotel elevator and bowed his head. "Man, that stuff is tiring," he said. "But the way I look at it, that's something I owe the game of basketball, which has given me so much. What's so hard about sitting around and answering questions? I want people to see the real me, and it's the press who portrays you. I want people, kids especially, to know that Michael

# CHAPTER 4

Jordan is a respectable young man. It's fun being the focal point of the team. You only go through life once, and you know all that stuff about going for the gusto. But, I don't want it to change my personality."

He made a bet during his rookie year with a Chicago sportswriter, swearing he would never get big-headed or cocky. The writer said if Michael did, the writer would write a headline story ripping him. Jordan agreed. It's a bet Jordan is still winning.

"I'm nothing that special," he said once while waiting in an airport for an early morning flight. "Sure, I play basketball better than some and can do some things on a court. But why do people react like that around me, like I'm some kind of a rock star or something?"

There was a freshness, a vitality, an exuberance in the rookie Jordan that has slowly worn away through the years. He was a frisky colt with the talent to win a Kentucky Derby long before his time. The spring in his legs was incredible. You watch him dunk today and he looks almost tired compared with that first year.

He was told by Julius Erving and many of the other stars to pace himself, not to burn out like some supernova. Jordan would listen thoughtfully, then a frown would crinkle up his forehead. How do you go about pacing yourself? Does that mean you don't go all-out on every play? It was inconceivable to this Peter Pan-like figure who loved playing so much he had a "Love of the Game" clause inserted in his contract. Teams discourage and often demand that their players avoid pickup games or unofficial, nonteam athletic activity for fear of injury. Michael's the kind of guy who could be walking down the street, see a bunch of guys having a ball in a playground and join right in on their game. The Bulls had no choice but to acquiesce.

That love of the game came through in everything Jordan did, which charmed a nation of basketball fans. When you paid your money to see him perform, you never came away disappointed. There was no half-steppin' in this man's world.

"I think he's an unbelievable person as well as a phenomenal basketball player," said Bulls assistant coach John Bach, a veteran of many NBA seasons. "It seems he can handle well the demands on his time that fall to a superstar, and can handle the game on the floor. And what's amazing is the vitality he brings to practice. He could be snobby about the whole affair, but he seems to love basketball above all. He doesn't let his money belt weigh him down. Let's face it. He makes so much out of open-court play and has an unbelievable talent of lift. When other players are reaching, he's lifting. He could be the best defensive player in the league when he feels like it. Anything you want, he does. When he turns on, he's unbelievable. And he has accepted that responsibility. He's not shirking it saying, 'I'm too tired; I'll just play offense.' That's what makes it so nice to be with Air Jordan airline. It flies every night."

The legend of Michael grew with every performance. Arenas that rarely sold out had

# CHAPTER 4

customers lined up for blocks hoping to get a ticket
to the Air Show. Even vandalism came into play. A
car parked in the Los Angeles Clippers parking lot
had two tickets stuck in the visor. A thief broke into
the car and stole the tickets. Only later did the
vandal realize the tickets were for a New Jersey Nets
game and not one of only two appearances Jordan
would make in Hollywood.

Those who attended Michael's debut at the L.A.
Memorial Sports Arena saw a move that Jordan has
not duplicated in his seven-year career. First, Jordan
hit a jumper to tie the Clippers at 100. With 1:26
left in the game, he smothered Norm Nixon
defensively and forced the Clipper star to shoot an
air ball. Caldwell Jones grabs the miss and unleashed
a two-handed pass.

Jordan caught up with the ball somewhere
beyond midcourt and began loading up for one of
his patented dunks. Derek Smith caught Jordan from
behind and wrapped him up in a bear hug as Jordan
was in midair. Somehow, with amazing grace,
Jordan was able to get off a shot while crash-
landing, unable even to see the basket. Two points,
foul, free throw good. Bulls win.

The capacity crowd stared in stunned disbelief,
then began chanting "USA, USA" in tribute to
Jordan's Olympian heroics in their city several
months earlier. "In Michael we trust," said assistant
coach Fred Carter. "All others pay cash."

Larry Bird became a believer after an early
meeting, a 110-106 Boston Celtic win at a sold-out
Chicago Stadium. "I have never seen one player

# RARE ROOKIE

turn around a team like that," Bird told the *Chicago Tribune* and snapped his fingers. "All the Bulls have become better because of him and pretty soon, this place will be packed every night, not just when the Celtics come to town. They'll pay just to watch Jordan. Got to.

"Best," Bird continued after watching Jordan finish with 41 points, 12 rebounds, and seven assists. "Never seen anyone like him. Unlike anyone I've ever seen. Phenomenal. One of a kind. He's the best. Ever." Even better that Larry Bird? "Yup. At this stage in his career, he's doing more than I ever did. I couldn't do what he did as a rookie. Heck, there was one drive tonight. He had the ball up in his right hand, then he took it down, then he brought it back up. I got a hand on it, fouled him and he still scored. And all the while he's in the air. You have to play this game to know how difficult that is. You see that and figure, 'Well, what the heck can you do?'"

Some inventive NBA stars apparently found a way to stop him. There was a huge controversy during the NBA All-Star game in Indianapolis when Jordan was the first rookie voted to start since Isiah Thomas in 1982. He was asked by Nike to wear a warmup outfit the company was promoting during the first two rounds of the Slam-Dunk Contest, during which Jordan finished second to Atlanta's Dominique Wilkins. Jordan cooperated, smiling all the while. Apparently, several players interpreted this act as a cocky gesture by the rookie. Who does this kid think he is? That sentiment mixed with a

# CHAPTER 4

Michael drives to the basket. Milwaukee guard Mike
Dunleavy, now the Lakers coach, said, "Very few rookies can
come into the NBA and dominate like this kid."

growing jealousy that Jordan was being marketed so
fabulously by his management group, ProServ,
primarily by the sharp and creative-thinking David
Falk. Michael was getting the attention, the perks,
the adoration, and the glamour that others thought
they deserved long ago.

Allegedly to teach the rookie a lesson, a story
circulated that Isiah Thomas, George Gervin, and
Magic Johnson plotted to freeze Jordan out of the
All-Star Game action and make him look bad on
national TV. Writers covering the game agreed there
were many times when Jordan flashed through the
middle wide open and nobody would pass him the
ball. Another reason for the alleged freeze-out was
that Jordan supposedly snubbed Thomas on a hotel
elevator. There was another rumor that because
Jordan would not listen to Thomas's financial
adviser—Dr. Charles Tucker, who also helped
manage Magic and Mark Aguirre and reportedly
wanted to steer Jordan away from ProServ—Michael
had to be punished.

One writer from Detroit said: "The attitude of
the players was Michael Jordan will get star
treatment when he learns how to act like a
gentleman."

"That makes me feel very small," Jordan told
the *Tribune.* "The whole thing has hurt me, really
hit me hard. I want to crawl into a hole and not
come out. I'll go home and mope the rest of the
day. I don't want to be perceived as having an
arrogant attitude."

What gave the rumors some credibility was the

report from a Detroit sportswriter that while walking through the airport, he saw Thomas, Gervin, Magic, and Tucker sitting together laughing. When asked about it, Tucker told the *Detroit Free Press:* "We were laughing about how they got Jordan."

Jordan hid his true feelings from the press and public. The day after the incident, however, while getting ready to play the Pistons and Isiah 24 hours later, you could tell Jordan was angry. While riding a stationary bicycle at a casual speed, he was asked about Thomas. The more Michael talked, the faster he pedaled until he was going at a furious rate. "I won't forget what happened or who did it to me," Jordan said behind a sweat-drenched scowl. The next night, playing like a man possessed, Jordan lit up the Pistons for 49 points en route to a 139-126 Bulls' overtime win. He again approached the 50-mark when the Bulls faced San Antonio and Gervin.

Jordan and Magic Johnson never got along in Michael's rookie year. Jordan always thought perhaps Magic was a little envious of this freshman coming in and stealing his thunder. Jordan tried explaining his feeling to a Chicago sportswriter, even using an incident in Los Angeles to support his claim. As the Bulls were preparing to take the Forum for a practice the day before their game with the Lakers, Magic & Co. were walking towards their locker rooms. The paths of the two teams crossed. Former Carolina teammate and buddy James Worthy was the first to greet Jordan with a big hug. Several other Lakers nodded their hellos. Magic was one of the last to walk by.

# RARE ROOKIE

"Watch this," Jordan told the reporter. "See if I'm not mistaken. I'll say 'hi' to Magic, and watch what happens." When Johnson had walked within five feet of him, Jordan smiled and said: "Hi, Magic." With a serious look on his face, Johnson never turned his face, never slowed his pace. He kept walking straight ahead, refusing to acknowledge the rookie. "See what I mean," Jordan said, a little confused.

Jordan wound up averaging more than 28 points a game, third-best in the league, and was among the league leaders in steals. He was named Rookie of the Year and deluged with endorsement offers that increased his bankroll by $5 million.

Jordan's second season was one of tumult that culminated in the single greatest individual postseason performance in NBA history. It all started when Jordan fractured a bone in his foot the third game of the season at Golden State. He missed 64 games, costing the Bulls an estimated $1.5 million in ticket revenue and costing the league one of its biggest attractions.

Yet nothing could keep him down. Sticking to his rehabilitation schedule religiously, Jordan felt healthy enough to sneak down to his beloved North Carolina four months later and secretly begin playing ball and testing the foot in pickup games with childhood and college friends. Then he made his stand.

The Bulls wanted to play it safe, let him sit out the season and come back completely healthy and strong for the 1986-87 season. The competitive

# CHAPTER 4

Jordan wanted no part of it. Although the club was floundering under coach Stan Albeck and acquiring Gervin in a trade wasn't nearly enough to compensate, Jordan thought he could still lead the team to a playoff berth.

The Bulls kept saying no, and Jordan got angrier every minute. Finally, one afternoon after a practice, he exploded. He ripped the Bulls management, saying it was intentionally trying to lose games so the club would wind up in the draft lottery and snare a top collegian. They were bitter accusations that made the front page of every sports section in town and, in some cases, led off the 10 o'clock news. It was behavior totally foreign to the superstar. Most times, the headline acts will simply collect their fat paychecks and plan for the future. Not Jordan. He continued his onslaught until owner Jerry Reinsdorf finally agreed to a special consultation with medical specialists from two different states.

In what has now come to be remembered as the extraordinary midnight press conference, Reinsdorf, Jordan, team physician Dr. John Hefferon, and the two specialists conducted a conference call and then met with the media sometime after midnight. Final verdict: Jordan would play, but only in small increments. It would start with seven minutes a half and gradually increase.

It forced Albeck to coach with a calculator and a stopwatch, trying to save the precious moments when he could use Jordan. It was frustrating for Jordan, who would often have to leave a game right at the most crucial moment because his allotted time was up. Albeck once tried to play him a minute longer to win a game and was threatened with being fired by general manager Jerry Krause if it ever happened again.

Finally, after playing like the Michael Jordan of old, Reinsdorf rescinded the time limit. It was the Bulls' final home game, and they needed a win to clinch a playoff berth. They trailed the Bullets at halftime when Reinsdorf announced during the intermission that Jordan was unchained. The Stadium crowd roared its approval and Jordan led the Bulls into the playoffs. With all that inactivity, Jordan was fresh compared to the tired athletes who had just completed an 82-game grind. That's one reason Albeck thought he had a chance to sneak up on the Celtics, who had the best record in basketball.

There was no way the Bulls could match up with Boston's Larry Bird, Kevin McHale, Robert Parish, Dennis Johnson, and Danny Ainge. Albeck instead used an old playground trick. His strategy called for the Bulls to transform the game into a two-on-two contest, Jordan and Orlando Woolridge against the two best Celtics.

It almost worked. In game one of the best-of-five series, Jordan rocked and rolled through Boston Garden for 49 points in a 123-104 loss. He had 30 points by halftime, the polite applause of fierce Boston partisans, and the Celtics more than a little worried. "Jordan did a very good job of wrecking our defensive plan and our offensive plan," Boston

# CHAPTER 4

coach K.C. Jones told the *Tribune*. "When a guy opens the game hitting five shots in a row, fear becomes a great factor on defense. That breaks down your thinking. It takes two or three minutes to adjust because the guy burned you so much. That's how bad he can make you look. Want to know how great Jordan is? Normally, the guys on the bench are leaning forward, trying to make eye contact with me. When they saw what Jordan was doing, nobody wanted in to guard him. I'd look down the bench and they were all leaning way back. So, I leaned back, too. When somebody went in, it took so long for their warmups to come off."

That proved to be just a preview for game two. It would be day basketball fans will never forget. There was a look on Jordan's face this Sunday that said he would not be denied this time. If he had to beat the Celtics one-on-five, so be it. Michael almost did. Jordan scored a playoff-record 63 points in a 135-131 double-overtime loss that pitted the game's best individual talent against the best team. The Celtics would go on to sweep the Bulls and eventually claim the NBA title, but as long-time Boston writer Bob Ryan would later observe, the closest Boston came to losing a home playoff game was to Michael and the Bulls.

Jordan hit off shots and regularly took three and four Celtics to the hoop. In one memorable sequence, he dribbled between his legs and then around Bird, shot by Dennis Johnson, took off over Kevin McHale, and double-pumped a layup with Robert Parish flailing away helplessly. One against four and Jordan wins.

Jordan sent the game into the first overtime by hitting two free throws with no time showing on the clock. "I was hoping he'd miss, but I knew he wouldn't," Jones said. "Players like him can will the ball in."

Michael had a chance to win it with three seconds left in the first extra session, but his 15-footer bounced off the rim. "I was thinking about North Carolina-Georgetown when you took that shot," Sidney Green told him, reviving memories of the NCAA tournament championship game-winner when Jordan was but a freshman. "[Jordan's performance against the Celtics] was incredible," Woolridge told the *Chicago Tribune*. "I just wish I could've been a spectator and sat back and watched. Being on the court with him, you could tell there was something magical happening."

Bird came away so impressed, he uttered the famous "I think he's God disguised as Michael Jordan" quote. "No question he had control of the game," Bird said to the *Tribune*. "He had to have one of the greatest feelings you can ever have. And, as hard as it might be to believe, it's actually fun playing against a guy like that. One thing I really like about him is that he said he was ready to play, even though management said no. He fought to come back. There was no question management wanted to get into the draft lottery. I think that takes a lot of guts. It shows you what kind of a person he is. You've got to feel happy for people like that."

# CHAPTER 5

# Offensive Force

*Left:* Michael shoots a jumper during his 61-point, 10-rebound, and four-steal performance in a 117-114 loss to the Atlanta Hawks. That was the game during which Michael scored an NBA-record 23 points in a row and when he scored his 3,000th point of the season.

# CHAPTER 5

WHAT THOSE FORTUNATE enough to have had tickets witnessed in 1986-87 is probably the most electrifying, crowd-pleasing individual season in the history of the game. When Michael Jordan became the first NBA player in 24 years to crack the 3,000-point barrier, it was accomplished with the kind of flair and drama that Wilt Chamberlain could never hope to match.

Chamberlain was a powerful 7'1" center who dominated an era when most pivot men were three and four inches shorter. The man nicknamed "The Big Dipper" mostly stood close to the basket and simply outmuscled his defenders. Not to take anything away from him, for he had incredible athletic talent for a man his size, but experts agree he wouldn't dominate in the same way if he were playing in the NBA today.

When a 6'6" guard scores 3,041 points, everyone takes notice. Michael's 1986-87 average of 37.1 points a game led the league, beginning a run of five consecutive scoring titles in five years (from 1986-87 to the 1990-91 season). He accomplished it in the face of double- and triple-teaming defenses combined with other "anti-Air" strategies. Jordan was surrounded by the likes of Earl Cureton, Brad Sellers, Granville Waiters, and Gene Banks—not exactly dangerous offensive threats. Michael did, however, have with him trusty outside-shooting guard John Paxson and rebounder supreme Charles Oakley.

The 1986-87 season was the year Jordan would forge an identity that would be fire-branded into the

Michael showed his vertical ability back as a prep player for Laney High School in Wilmington, North Carolina.

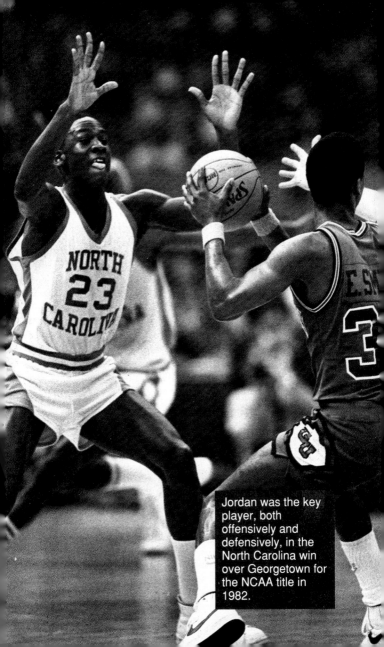

Jordan was the key player, both offensively and defensively, in the North Carolina win over Georgetown for the NCAA title in 1982.

Presenting his "air" moves worldwide, Michael proudly delivered a gold medal to the US team in the '84 Olympics.

*Above:* Bulls head coach Doug Collins (right) encourages Jordan during Michael's MVP year of 1987-88. *Below:* Michael brings the ball up the floor. He is so versatile that he plays all-star quality point guard, two guard, and small forward.

Not just a scoring machine, Jordan led the NBA in steals two straight seasons and was the 1987-88 Defensive Player of the Year.

Michael won his first Slam Dunk contest in 1987, using the shot that forever validated Jordan's skywalking abilities.

*Above:* Generous with his time almost to a fault, Michael will sign autographs for kids for hours. *Below:* The most famous pair of basketball shoes in the world.

The Michael Jordan Foundation is a non-profit organization that organizes Michael's charitable efforts.

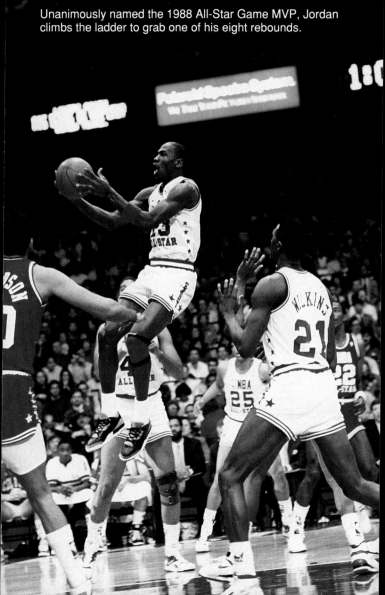

Unanimously named the 1988 All-Star Game MVP, Jordan climbs the ladder to grab one of his eight rebounds.

*Above:* When Michael is given the smallest seam, he will drive to the hoop all day. *Below:* Of course, Jordan is equally effective driving to an open spot on the floor and dishing to a wide-open teammate.

Jordan is not able to be intimidated and will make his anger known, as Charlotte's Kelly Tripucka finds out.

Michael is the ultimate "go-to" guy. Here he shoots a last-second shot against the Knicks in the 1989 playoffs.

*Above:* Celebrating his 26th birthday, Michael serves his father, James, some cake while his mother, Deloris, looks on. *Below:* Michael has said that he hopes to join the PGA Tour or the Seniors Circuit after his basketball days are over.

Baseball was Jordan's first love. During a recent promotion with the ChiSox, he showed Strawberry-esque form at bat.

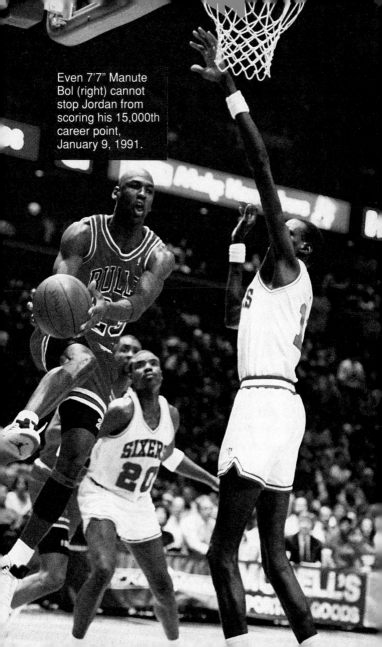

Even 7'7" Manute Bol (right) cannot stop Jordan from scoring his 15,000th career point, January 9, 1991.

Michael slams another "Hollywood Show Time" monster jam against the Lakers in La-La Land.

# OFFENSIVE FORCE

psyches of opposing coaches and players who tried to contain him. It was almost as if he was returning to the NBA with a vengeance after having missed 64 games the previous year with the broken left foot.

All the great games and outrageously terrific moves Jordan had made would be eclipsed during this season. When he scored the 63 points in the playoff loss to Boston the year before, it was foreshadowing—ominous to those who played against him, joyful for those who wore the Bulls' colors.

Have your calculator ready as we take you through the highest-scoring season an NBA player will have for a long, long time.

Appropriately enough, Jordan's assault on the record books began on opening night at Madison Square Garden, the media capital of America. New coach Doug Collins had won over his players with an emotional style that would have them hustling all 82 games. Jordan wanted to make Collins's baptism into the NBA special, so Michael went out and lit up the Knicks for 50 points to make Collins a winner on his first try. In an emotional scene as the final horn sounded, Collins and Jordan embraced, and then the coach went on to hug all his players. If you looked closely, you could see the tears beginning to well up in Collins's eyes. Later, he would describe Jordan's offense as a "nuclear weapon."

"What he's done is incredible," said Knicks' coach Hubie Brown. "We had Rory Sparrow in [Jordan's] face the last seven minutes, but he did things that were astounding. He had a couple of

# CHAPTER 5

shots off the glass that were unbelievable. You say: 'How the hell did he get that off?' But not only does he get it off, but it backspins in like a feather. He was magic. Whatever arena he goes to, people are flocking to see him play."

Jordan went on a tear before midseason and accomplished a feat that hadn't been done in 25 years. He scored 40 or more points in nine straight games. Most pro players would be ecstatic to score 40 once. Twice in that span, he scored 50. When Jordan puts it all together—the floating-in-air hang time, the rocket-quick, explosive first step, hands the same size as 7'2" Artis Gilmore, the acrobatic moves, Elgin Baylor-like body control, and the outside jumper—the Department of Defense would have a difficult time shooting him down.

It was all working the night of January 8 when he scored what was then a regular-season high 53 points in a 121-117 victory over the Portland Trail Blazers. One move was unforgettable. Late in the game, Jordan posted up another all-pro, Clyde Drexler, and when Blazer teammate Jim Paxson came over to double-team, Michael kicked his act into high gear. He exploded past both of them, took off, and was gliding across the lane when Caldwell Jones and Jerome Kersey joined the chase. No matter, because Jordan flew past them and scored with an over-the-shoulder, reverse layup. One against four is not an even matchup when that one is Air Jordan.

"I just felt that any shot, because of the way things were flowing, was going in," Jordan told the

# OFFENSIVE FORCE

*Chicago Tribune.* "This is the type of game where your instincts take over. There was no hesitating, no thinking. The natural talents just flowed through. That's when you really feel it. I could've taken a half-court shot and it would be all net. I was really motivated tonight. I knew we had a chance to go two games above .500. I felt this was the first time I had to lead the team to get them motivated. We came out a little flat, and I told them: 'Come on, guys, let's get going. We're dragging our butts. There's 11,000 people out there and we're playing one of the worst games of the seasons.'"

Getting Jordan motivated is never problem, but the Philadelphia 76ers' enfant terrible, Charles Barkley, found a way to set off Air Jordan even higher than usual. The two superstars have since become good friends and at times have playfully grabbed one another or held onto a jersey during a game, with the victim responding with a good-natured hand slap and a smile.

On a Saturday night in January 1987, before they had gotten to know one another, Barkley uttered a contemptuous challenge to Jordan. It was more like the hype before a heavyweight championship fight than a pregame basketball comment. "I won't let Michael Jordan score 40 points if I have to break him up into little pieces," Barkley told the *Chicago Tribune* upon entering Chicago Stadium.

"I'd advise him to worry about the game," Jordan responded back to the *Tribune.* "The only thing he can do is speak for himself. Whatever he says doesn't matter. I'll just put it out of my mind. He doesn't set the tone for my motivation. I guess he wants to try and take me out of my game. I won't let him do that. I won't let him rattle me."

Not only did Jordan pick up the gauntlet, but he threw it back in Prince Charles's face with 47 points, 10 rebounds, and six assists in a 105-89 blowout of the visitors from Philly. After the game? "I was just kidding when I said that," Barkley said to the *Tribune*. "But I didn't want him to score a lot of points and embarrass us." Barkley was then

Jordan scored 50 or more points eight times in 1986-87, and only one other player, Wilt Chamberlain, had scored 50 or more points in three consecutive games.

asked to compare Jordan to Julius Erving, the
renowned Dr. J. "To me, there is no comparison,"
Barkley responded to the *Tribune*. "Doc is much
better. He's the most talented athlete to ever play
the game."

In the other locker room, Jordan told the
*Tribune* his side of the story. "Barkley kind of got
me going when he said he would keep me not only
under 40, but under my average of 37 points, and
that he would 'break me' if I went over 37. I think
all he was trying to do was take my mind away from
the game. But all I did was block it out and play as
hard as I could."

Opponents tried everything from Barkley-esque
intimidation to sweet talk, praising Jordan to the
high heavens in hopes of lulling him into some sense
of complacency. Nothing worked. He shredded the
76er defense 12 days later for 49 points in the
Spectrum in a 121-112 loss to the Sixers. That
night, he set an arena record for the most points in a
regular season game. Just to make certain 76er fans
realized it wasn't a fluke, Jordan returned on March
11 and again scored 49. Whether he was spurred on
by Barkley's comments, Jordan seemed to sharpen
his game up whenever he went against Barkley &
Co. In a 93-91 win at the Stadium before a
standing-room-only crowd of 18,122, Michael scored
56 points, hitting 22 of 32 shots with eight steals
and seven rebounds.

While Michael was hot all that season, he was
feeling the blues one time during a cold, dreary
February day. In Chicago, it was 20 degrees with

# CHAPTER 5

about four inches of snow on the ground. In need of some cheering up, Jordan called his mom in North Carolina after practice. MJ said that the weather was getting to him and that it wasn't "any place for a Carolina boy." Deloris said that it was 75 degrees in Wallace. Michael said: "I'm coming home. Fix me my favorite for dinner."

With that, Jordan hopped on a plane, arrived back home in time to get in a quick 18 holes of golf, had a sumptuous dinner with the family, and caught a late-night flight back to Chicago. Jordan had a king-sized smile on his face the next day in practice as he whistled while he worked. His teammates noticed the extra zeal in his play and wondered what happened. When he told them, they just shook their heads and smiled. "That's Michael for ya," seemed to be their collective thought.

Back on the floor, this young multimillionaire began to stretch the limits of credibility, as Jordan put on a scoring exhibition that delighted fans everywhere. On a Friday night in February, he bombarded the New Jersey Nets for 58 points, breaking by two points the Bulls' regular-season record for points in a game held by Chet Walker since 1972. In dropping 26 of 27 free throws, Michael shattered the club mark of 25 held by Artis Gilmore. Jordan had 34 points by halftime, finishing with 11 in the third quarter and 13 in the fourth as the Bulls ran away from the Nets 128-113.

"I think he's the best offensive player I've seen," Indiana Pacer coach Jack Ramsay told the *Indianapolis Star.* "Just creatively with the ball,

# OFFENSIVE FORCE

he's probably the best ever. When he gets to the basket, he's tough because he's in the air. It's tough to defend a player in the air. You're not going to block his shot. In defensing him, there's nobody like him. Everybody's different, and everybody has a different game. Larry Bird and Magic Johnson require their special games, but Jordan is in a class by himself in that respect."

Twice, Jordan would reach the 61-point mark, once against the Detroit Pistons and once against the Atlanta Hawks, which culminated a sensational three-game stretch. The final week of the season began with Michael burning the Pacers for 53 points, eight assists, and four steals in a 116-95 win on April 12. He hit 14 of his first 18 shots in a performance that left the guys from Indiana shell-shocked.

The very next night, he went off for 50 points, nine rebounds, four steals, and three blocked shots in a 114-107 win over the Bucks in Milwaukee. He completed this trifecta of Michael-mania three nights later with a 61-point, 10-rebound, and four-steal performance in a 117-114 loss to the Atlanta Hawks. The 61 points tied the club record he had set earlier against the Pistons.

Only one other player, Wilt Chamberlain, had scored 50 or more points in three consecutive games. That was also the game that elevated Michael into the rarified air of the 3,000-point club. He also scored an NBA-record 23 points in a row, eclipsing the old record of 18 straight he had set earlier in the season.

# CHAPTER 5

In scoring 23 points nonstop, Jordan had scored 50 or more points for the eighth time that season. Most NBA players never score 50 in their careers. All-time greats Elgin Baylor and Rick Barry, a pair of prolific scorers, scored 50 points 17 and 14 times, respectively, in their careers. Barry, a Hall-of-Famer, who works as a TV analyst, said: "In all my basketball fantasies over the years, I never dreamed the things Michael Jordan actually does. They say all men are created equally, but that was before God created Michael Jordan."

Yet, Michael is still the same guy whose idea of a gourmet meal is Chicken McNuggets and a Coke. He loves junk food. His pregame meal is a ritual he adheres to religiously. For games that start at the normal time of 7:30 p.m., Jordan will have a meal of steak and eggs precisely at 4 p.m. On the road, when he can duck out into a shopping mall restaurant off the beaten path, he'll ask for a table in a completely secluded section and sometimes can eat a meal like a normal person. Most times, he'll simply order room service. He registers in hotels under an assumed name to avoid causing a commotion.

The public fell in love with Michael, a love affair that grows more passionate with every game. Kids and grownups sense a certain humility about him, that he has doesn't feel he's any better than the next man and, personality-wise at least, can fit right in with the common folks.

He was sitting in an airport terminal one afternoon that season, awaiting a commercial flight with his teammates. This was during spring vacation and hundreds of school kids were making their way to various destinations. All it took was one of them to spot Jordan and before long, hundreds had mobbed him seeking an autograph or just wanting to reach out and shake his hand. Watching this, a flight attendant offered Jordan the sanctuary of a private office until the plane was ready to take off. "No, that's okay," Jordan replied. "I'll just stay here and sign these autographs. The way I look at it, this is just a small thing I can give back to a game that has given me so much."

Jordan isn't afraid of his public. During a discussion with a sportswriter that season, he shared his feelings on using drugs, a discussion prompted by the story that New York Mets pitcher Dwight Gooden had just tested positive for cocaine.

"I'm not afraid of what I've become," Jordan told the *Chicago Tribune*. "I don't think of it [adulation] as pressure. I think of it as a compliment. Maybe it's because I didn't have the type of growing up that most superstars have. I came on so suddenly and quickly, a late bloomer. I didn't have time to see myself in this situation. It's helped me to act more naturally."

Both Jordan and Gooden had images of the clean-cut athlete until Gooden succumbed to his own personal demons. When Jordan was asked if the same could happen to him, his voice quivered at times as he answered. "I scored 13 points against Washington last month and it was the worst game I've played in the NBA," he said. "That could've been the perfect time to go out and get drunk or get

# CHAPTER 5

involved with something I'm not supposed to.
Instead, I had dinner with my attorney, David Falk,
and a friend, David Robinson, the Navy center. I
blocked it out of my mind. I know I'm only human.
And I've got that inner confidence to put that
behind me and know it can't last forever.

"I'm so positive that I can look within myself to
find something positive instead of looking around for
things I shouldn't do to get my confidence back. I'm
not scared. Every human being makes mistakes, and
his mistakes came back to haunt him. My lifestyle is
so positive that I'm not afraid of something from my
past coming back to haunt me or upset the role-
model image I've set. I live a clean, healthy life, and
I'm happy about it. I've never done drugs, and I'll
never have a reason to do drugs." Jordan was told
the story of how Gooden was once upset by a fan
who went up to him in a restaurant, took the fork
out of his hand, stuck a pen there, and requested an
autograph. Gooden's response was one of anger.
"You have to accept that," Jordan said. "There are
some things you have to give up when you become a
superstar. Someone like Gooden or myself goes to a
restaurant and gets seated faster than the average
person. We get free food or someone pays for our
meals. To get those added attractions, you have to
give something up."

During this season, Jordan began rubbing
elbows with the biggest celebrities. *60 Minutes*
interviewed him, filming a segment with Jordan and
correspondent Diane Sawyer playing a game of one-
on-one before the interview. "I wondered, 'is there

anything wrong with him?'" *60 Minutes* producer
Bill Brown said. "The answer is, nothing. [Jordan] is
absolutely a young man totally at ease with destiny.
He is comfortable with his role as a superstar. He is
also very alert to the possibilities of the pressures on
him. He is totally comfortable with his role in life.
Even if his celebrity went away, he would be
comfortable with himself. The extraordinary athletic
prowess, the sudden fame, an instant millionaire, and
yet, here is this kid still unaffected."

This was also the season he graced the cover of
*GQ* magazine and outpolled Magic Johnson as the
No. 1 vote-getter in the fans' All-Star balloting.
Michael won his first NBA Slam-Dunk Contest,
dividing the $12,500 prize money among his
teammates. "It's very rare for a player to share his
winnings with his teammates," said Clyde Drexler,
who also competed. "He's a classy guy. I wish he
was on my team. I've never heard of a basketball
player doing this. It's good to see a guy with a kind
heart." Bulls teammate Gene Banks said, "He's a
genuine individual, one in a million. He's one of
God's special children."

"I'm very happy with my season," Jordan said.
"I'm surprised I scored this many points, and I
don't think I'll ever have another season like this
offensively."

As he walked out of the Stadium locker room
for the final time in that memorable season after the
Celtics had swept the Bulls 3-0 in the playoffs,
Jordan glanced back and said: "You know, maybe
this will be the greatest season I ever have."

# Most Valuable Player

*Left:* During Jordan's first MVP season, he became the first player in NBA history to win the scoring title (35 points a game) and be named Defensive Player of the Year in the same season. He also led the league in steals (3.16 a game), and averaged 5.5 rebounds and 5.9 assists per game.

# CHAPTER 6

AFTER THE 1987–88 CAMPAIGN, a panel of select nationwide media finally came to their collective senses and gave Michael Jordan his due. No. 23 finally became No. 1. Jordan finally was voted the NBA's MVP.

This had been a raging debate ever since Jordan led the league with 37.1 points a game the previous year. It was easy for detractors and those in the media to dismiss him as a gunner. Yet, argued the pro-Jordan forces, clarify your specifications for the Award and Michael will be the prime candidate in every instance.

There was no denying Jordan after a precedent-setting season. Does one measure an MVP according to how valuable he is to his team? Well, Jordan was simply the Bulls' best offensive player, best defensive player, second-best rebounder, one of the best passers, best in steals, best in blocked shots, and was the reason an average of 18,000 Chicagoans were flocking to Chicago Stadium. If needed, Michael could have sold popcorn and swept up afterwards. If Jordan isn't valuable, then neither are the security guards at Fort Knox. Jordan was highly thought of enough to be one of five new entries in the 1988 *World Book Encyclopedia.*

San Francisco Giants manager Roger Craig was asked to pick one athlete outside of baseball he'd like to suit up. "Michael Jordan," Craig told the *San Francisco Examiner.* "He's one of the best athletes I've ever seen. I'd put him in center field. He'd have great range out there, and he could jump into the second deck to catch home runs. And, he could

# MOST VALUABLE PLAYER

hit for power. He'd be like Willie Mays—a guy who can do everything."

Jordan once made a promotional appearance in Pittsburgh and then was asked to throw out the first ball at the Pirates' season opener. When he entered Three Rivers Stadium, he reduced even big league ballplayers to admiring fans. Many of the Pirate players and manager Jim Leyland asked him to autograph a baseball. After the first-ball ceremony as he was walking off the field, an umpire stopped him and asked for an autograph. Maybe the term Most Valuable doesn't quite get it. Maybe the league should invent yet another award, a higher category, like "Most Precious Player." After all, it was former Atlanta Hawks public relations director Bill Needle who once described Jordan as a "national treasure."

Since Bird and Magic had dominated the MVP Award in the 1980s, Jordan was most often compared to them. The argument against Jordan was that Bird and Magic made the players around them better, therefore they won championships and were more valuable. The Jordanites countered that Bird's and Magic's teammates were already accomplished pros, some all-pros, while Jordan labored with blue-collar guys. Indeed, according to coach Doug Collins, "the Bulls without Michael Jordan would be the L.A. Clippers." Perhaps Jordan's running mate, guard John Paxson, had the solution. "Magic and Bird are the best players in the game who play *on the floor,*" Paxson said. "Michael is the best player in the game who plays *in the air.*"

Jordan was untouchable in his fourth season. In a

league full of thoroughbreds, he was Secretariat. He
became the first player in NBA history to win the
scoring title (35 points a game) and be named
Defensive Player of the Year in the same season.
That was just the beginning. He led the league in
steals (3.16 a game), blocked more shots than 16
starting centers, was first-team all-NBA and all-
defense, was the league's slam-dunk champion, and
became the only player ever to block 100 shots and
record 200 steals in consecutive seasons. He also
reached four NBA and eight club playoff records
and became the first player to score 50 points in
consecutive playoff games.

Michael Jordan (right) and John Paxson helped the Bulls to
a 50-win season, the team's best record since the
1973-74 season.

# MOST VALUABLE PLAYER

What is "Most Valuable?" Is Jordan's accounting
for 35 percent of the Bulls' offense considered
valuable? Somewhere along the way, the NBA media
had been missing something. There could be a
natural bias at work here in that scoring champions
rarely win the MVP Award because they're
perceived as being selfish players. The path Jordan
took to his first Most Valuable Player Award was a
fascinating one. The Bulls would enjoy their first 50-
win season in 14 years and finally enter the upper
echelon of the league. The average attendance, which
was 6,365 in the pre-Jordan era, rocketed to 18,060
in 1987-88. Primarily because of Jordan, the Bulls
hauled in an estimated $10 million in ticket revenue.
Jordan also continued filling the coffers of other
NBA teams, selling out arenas wherever he went.
Once in Houston at an off-day promotion, Jordan
was supposed to sign autographs for 300 fans. Word
spread and 5,000 showed up. When it became
apparent that they would get nowhere near the man
to get his signature, people resorted to mob action,
storming over tables and crashing through barriers to
get at Jordan. A security team just barely got him
away safely.

Jordan chose an auspicious way to open the
season. He bolted out of a preseason practice 20
minutes before Collins blew the final whistle. It was
the first time Michael, always Mr. Clean, had done
anything bearing a hint of the unsavory. A
sportswriter who was acquainted with Michael
followed him home. In his kitchen, munching on
Kentucky Fried Chicken, Jordan unleashed all his

pent-up frustration.

Ostensibly, the brouhaha was about Collins making a mistake on the score of a scrimmage in which the losers would run extra laps after practice. Jordan claimed what angered him was Collins's refusal simply to recheck the correct score with the players. While on the record, Jordan was cautious with his comments. Repeatedly, he asked the writer to put away his pen and pad so he could come clean off the record. Finally, the notepad was shut and Jordan opened up. He had some serious doubts about Collins and the type of leadership he was showing. Jordan felt the pressure was beginning to wear thin on the aggressive young coach. He was upset Collins was continuing two-a-day workouts when Michael didn't believe it was doing the team any good. He had been late to practice twice that week, saying he had overslept from the exhaustion of Collins's regimen. When Collins had shouted at guard Sedale Threatt during a preseason game, Jordan had said something back in defense of his teammate. Collins was not the kind of coach who would stand for having his authority challenged in the least.

"Have you noticed the changes in Dougie?" Jordan asked the writer, who was beginning his fourth season covering the Bulls for the *Chicago Tribune* and had been close to the scene in Collins's debut the year before. In a separate and equally private conversation, Collins indicated he thought Jordan was undergoing changes. As one might expect, the local sports radio talk shows conducted

# MOST VALUABLE PLAYER

phone-in balloting that ran heavily in Jordan's favor.
Neither spoke the entire next day, but on Thursday,
they settled their differences and Collins kissed
Jordan on the cheek in front of TV cameras.

Any conflict was soon lost in the blaze of the
Bulls' fast start. For the first three weeks of the
season, Jordan & Co. were the hottest team in pro
basketball. Their 4-0 start was the best in the Bulls'
22-year history. At 9-2, they had the NBA's best
record. They improved to 12-3 and such teams as
the Celtics and Lakers began wondering if they
would have to make room at the top.

With Charles Oakley beginning to assert himself
underneath and with the aging but at times effective
7'2" Artis Gilmore beginning his second tour of
duty in the Windy City, the Bulls took on a
formidable look. First-round draft choices Scottie
Pippen and Horace Grant would be erratic yet their
talent was undeniable. John Paxson was steady as
ever. In the opener before 18,688 fans at Chicago
Stadium, Jordan poured on 36 points, Oakley
collected 21 rebounds, and the Bulls whipped the
76ers 104-94.

While Dave Corzine was playing center for the
Bulls in the 1986-87 season, he and Jordan had an
ongoing argument about which was the greater feat:
Jordan's consuming 30 Chicken McNuggets at one
sitting or Corzine devouring 150 peel-and-eat
shrimp. Corzine claimed the chicken was more
impressive because of the grease and coating. Jordan
said Corzine's shrimp-fest was more than anything
he could ever top.

# CHAPTER 6

The two got along famously, the big, strong, white center and the quick, athletic, black shooting guard. Perhaps more than anyone, Jordan appreciated the sturdy picks and screens Corzine would set to free him. Corzine was fond of bragging about Jordan and was one of his biggest admirers. Jordan often said Corzine was one of the strongest players in the NBA and only his easygoing demeanor and slow temper prevented him from one day tearing someone apart. Little did Michael know that he would be the target of a rare Corzine outburst at a practice session during the 1987-88 season.

No one is certain quite how it began, although Jordan is well known for his jabbering during scrimmages and games. It could've been that Corzine came to the workout already in a bad mood and Jordan's playful taunts lit a slow fuse. There was some banging on one play, and suddenly Corzine shook free and began advancing towards Jordan. Backpedaling with the speed of a Sugar Ray Leonard in his prime, Jordan had his fists up for protection, but you could tell by the look on his face that he didn't want to resort to using them. Oakley and small forward Gene Banks, two strong individuals themselves, wrapped their arms around the big 6'11", 265-pound Corzine until he cooled down. Jordan had always said Corzine was one guy he wouldn't want to mess with if the big guy lost his temper. Yet, theirs was a relationship that if anybody else threatened Jordan with bodily harm, "Big Cor" was one of the first, along with Oakley, to take up his fight.

# MOST VALUABLE PLAYER

After the home opener came a staunch road test in Atlanta. Jordan issued a pregame challenge to the Hawks, saying it was about time the Bulls realized they were good enough to beat Dominique Wilkins's gang on its own turf. Jordan's comments found their way into an Atlanta newspaper, and the talented Hawks were riled. No matter, Jordan had 29 points, seven assists, and six steals in a 105-95 win. Road wins in the NBA are precious. The league just seems set up to let the good guys in the white uniforms win most of the time. So, when the Bulls followed the Atlanta success with a 105-96 win at New Jersey, the players themselves began wondering if this was all for real. They all knew Jordan was the real deal, but what about the rest of them? In looking back, experts agree Collins did a masterful job in turning the Bulls into a gang of high overachievers. Even though Jordan was the only one qualified to play in the air, everyone else began playing above their heads this season.

Back home, the Bulls routed the Nets 103-85, the fourth-straight time they'd held an opponent under 100. Jordan had a workmanlike 36 points, seven rebounds, and six steals. The Indiana Pacers came to town and the high-feeling Bulls may have overlooked this lowly bunch. Oakley created a critical turnover late in the game allowing Chuck Person to hit the winning basket in a 111-110 loss before 18,676 disappointed Bulls fans. Estimates after this tremendous turnaround for the Bulls at the turnstile revealed that because of Jordan alone, the Bulls probably made $7 million more than they would've if someone like Sam Bowie had been their pick in the '84 draft.

Kareem Abdul-Jabbar and the Lakers, and other top teams, had a tough time stopping Jordan and the Bulls.

# MOST VALUABLE PLAYER

The Bulls went to 6-1 when Oakley had 19 points and a monstrous 24 rebounds at Washington. Oakley grabbed more boards than anyone else in the league in 1987-88, but he would lose the rebound title on the last day to Seattle's Michael Cage, who played fewer games and had a slightly higher average. Despite an early season loss to the Pistons that was almost a foreshadowing of things to come, the Bulls continued to roll. They upset the Celtics 107-102 in Hartford, Connecticut, and followed with a 103-101 win in Milwaukee to give them an NBA-best 5-0 mark on the road.

Coming off that prolific scoring spree the year before, Jordan kept things low key until erupting for 47 points, nine assists, three steals, and three blocks in a rousing 105-101 win at Utah. Early in the third quarter, Jordan drove and dunked easily over 6'2" Jazz guard John Stockton. "Hey Jordan, why don't you pick on somebody your own size," shouted a Jazz courtside season ticketholder who loved to razz opposing teams. Jordan glanced over at him, making a mental note as he raced back upcourt. On the very next play, Jordan again came slashing towards the basket, this time slamming it over 7', 290-pound Melvin Turpin. As he ran upcourt, Jordan looked right at the Jazz fan and asked, "Is he big enough?" The fan shook his head and laughed and Jordan smiled.

Jordan was named the NBA's Player of the Month and Collins was honored as Coach of the Month as the Bulls won 12 of their first 15 games. The Bulls would eventually level off, but not No 23.

# CHAPTER 6

In a 111-100 victory over the Cleveland Cavaliers December 17 at the Stadium, Jordan racked up 52 points on 20 of 31 shooting, including an NBA-high at that time 30 points in the second half. More foreshadowing of what MJ later would do to the Cavs in the playoffs. Said Craig Ehlo who was defending Jordan: "I was handed my breakfast, lunch, and dinner all in one night."

In a raucous Stadium rumble on January 16, Jordan had 36 points, 10 rebounds, and 10 assists in a 115-99 win over the Pistons. During the game, a pair of 6'9" musclemen, Oakley and Rick Mahorn, squared off in a violent fight. Collins, who didn't always see eye-to-eye with Oakley, jumped into the fray and put a headlock around Mahorn. Incensed, Mahorn grabbed the Bulls coach and threw him over the scorer's table, where Bulls' TV analyst Johnny "Red" Kerr caught him. Undaunted, Collins launched himself back at Mahorn and was slugged in the face. By the time order was restored, a bruised Mahorn and a battered Oakley were ejected.

With the All-Star Game in Chicago, Jordan put on a critically acclaimed show for the home folks and a national TV audience. First, he successfully defended his slam-dunk title over runnerup Dominique Wilkins, relying on a free-throw line jam choreographed by Julius Erving and a "Kiss The Rim" slam that garnered a perfect score. The next day, he scored 40 points in leading the East to victory and was awarded the MVP trophy. More foreshadowing.

Jordan began revving up for a record-breaking

playoff scoring binge in the final two months of the regular season. He had 52 points in a loss to Portland and 50 in the Bulls' first Stadium win over the Celtics since December 17, 1985. After that game, Kevin McHale observed: "Jordan singlehandedly dismembered and dismantled all of us." On March 23, after scoring just 16 points in the first half and bristling from a Collins comment that "David Wingate is kicking your butt," Jordan scored 33 second-half points to Wingate's zero in a 118-102 win over Philly.

Then, in perhaps his best game of the regular season, Michael put up 59 points, hitting 20 of his first 24 shots, in a 112-110 win over the Pistons in the Silverdome. With 24 seconds left, Jordan blocked a shot by Isiah Thomas, and with four seconds to go, he hit the winning free throws. "He was on fire," Pistons guard Vinnie Johnson told the *Chicago Tribune*. "He was in his own little funk, and there was no way I could get him out of it. He hit a few shots that I know even he had to be impressed with himself. There was this one drive to the hole, and three of our guys jumped at him. We swiped at him, spun him around, fouled him, and it still fell in. We played him man-to-man in the first half, he scored 32 points. We tried double-teaming him in the second half, but by that time he was extremely hot. He felt like he could do anything out there, which is what he did." This may have provided the motivation for the Pistons eventually devising a defensive strategy later to be called "The Jordan Rules." It would come into play when the

# CHAPTER 6

two teams met in the second round of the playoffs.

Not long after, Jordan reached agreement with the Bulls on a new eight-year contract that would pay him $28 million. No wonder he was so charged up down the stretch. He had 47 points in a win over the Knicks, and in the season finale he scored 46 points in a clutch win over the Celtics. It gave Chicago the third-best record in the East, as Jordan clinched his second consecutive scoring title.

Jordan had a career playoff series in leading the Bulls past Cleveland 3-2. He had 50 points in the opener, a 104-93 win in which he equaled or set six club records. After burning Ehlo again, Jordan heard good friend and Cavs guard Ron Harper say that Michael would "never get 50 on me." In game two, Jordan against Harper, MJ goes off for 55 points in a 106-101 win. He was the first guy ever to do the 50-50 thing in successive postseason games. Between games, he shot a 75 at a Chicago area golf course. At that point he had broken or tied two NBA playoff records and 14 club marks.

Jordan had "only" 38 points and nine assists in the game three loss and was held to 44 when the Cavs evened the series. He had 39 and Pippen a playoff-high 24 in the decisive win back home. Jordan finished the series averaging an absurd 45.2 points a game when scoring is supposed to drop below regular-season standards. It's a record for a five-game series.

Pistons assistant coach Ron Rothstein is credited with designing the "Jordan Rules," 13 defensive sets to counter Jordan's favorite and most effective moves. What the Jordan Rules boil down to is that the Pistons double-teamed him before he got the ball, and when that wasn't possible, they forced him one way into a double-team trap. It worked in the opener as Jordan was limited to 29 points in a 93-82 Detroit win. Bulls guard Sam Vincent foiled the strategy in game two with 31 points as the Bulls won 105-95 and went home with the best-of-seven series even.

In game three, Detroit was the epitome of its bad-boy image. Just 1:37 into the game, Bill Laimbeer set an illegal screen into Jordan and was whistled for a foul. Jordan claims after the whistle Laimbeer intentionally elbowed Michael in the groin. Incensed, he took a swing at an opposing player for the first time in his career, missing with a right hook. A melee erupted, emotions flared, and the Bulls were never the same. Accustomed to such guerilla warfare, the Pistons swept both games in Chicago, 101-79 and 96-77. Jordan only scored 24 points in game three and 23 two days later. The Bulls were eliminated back in Pontiac, Michigan, 102-95 as Jordan had 25 points, eight rebounds, and eight assists. Still, something about him impressed Pistons coach Chuck Daly.

"He's Superman," Daly told the *Tribune.* "I don't know how he does it, where he gets that energy, his intelligence, his instinct for the game. It's like Philadelphia when Julius Erving was there. I'm telling the people of Chicago: 'You're seeing something there that only comes around once in a lifetime.'"

# Midas Touch

Left: Michael Jordan lines up his shot on the green. When not playing basketball, Jordan's schedule is filled to the brim with golf events. What both frustrates and fascinates Jordan is golf's unpredictability and how he can never control the game. He said that after he retires from the NBA, he wants to join the PGA Seniors Circuit.

# CHAPTER 7

**T**HERE IS SOMETHING UNIQUE about Michael Jordan, a presence that goes beyond the Baryshnikov-like hang time and the aerial ballet that have made him the best-known basketball player in the world.

It starts with his personality—warm, outgoing, genuine. Joking with him at his locker room stall, sitting with him in a restaurant, watching him shoot some pool in his basement, these are the times you come to know the real man. There doesn't seem to be anything artificial about the guy. He can afford to be anybody he wants to be, of course, with the millions of dollars fattening his bank account each year.

Michael's Midas touch begins with the Bulls' contract that will pay him an average of $3 million a year through 1995. Add onto that the estimated $7 million and climbing that he nets in endorsements each year. That makes him the highest-paid team-sport player in the marketing world, not yet in the neighborhood of someone such as golfer Arnold Palmer, who brings in more than $20 million in endorsements. Michael's clients include McDonald's, Coca-Cola, Wheaties, Nike, Chevrolet, Wilson Sporting Goods, Guy La Rouche watches, Johnson Products, several clothing firms, and others. He also has limited real estate partnerships in Miami; Kansas City; San Clemente, California; and Washington, D.C. He also owns land in Hilton Head, South Carolina. His appeal is so strong that his mother, Deloris, now appears on commercials for Empire Carpeting in Chicago.

# MIDAS TOUCH

Michael is represented by ProServ, a Washington, D.C.-based sports management group. ProServ senior vice president David Falk has been overseeing Jordan's financial empire from day one. Rather than the shotgun approach taken by other huge sports celebrities, such as Bears coach Mike Ditka, Falk advocated carefully selecting only those corporations and products that best reflect the image Jordan portrays. In the case of McDonald's, Jordan does swear by the fast-food conglomerate. He's been consuming Big Macs since he was old enough to walk up to the counter.

He had just finished a workout with the 1984 Olympic team when coach Bobby Knight came in and told several of the players they'd been drafted by NBA teams. He asked them how they would commemorate such an occasion and most of the players said they'd be dining at expensive restaurants, running up exorbitant tabs and toasting with Dom Perignon. Jordan was strangely silent. "Well Jordan, you were the third player picked. What are you going to do to celebrate?" Knight asked Jordan. "I'm going down to McDonald's and ordering three Big Macs, with fries and a large Coke," Michael said with a grin. According to Knight, that's exactly what the North Carolina star did. It's little wonder McDonald's came out with a "limited edition" of the "McJordan" burger, a sandwich with a hamburger patty, two strips of bacon, barbecue sauce, and all the trimmings.

"Michael Jordan continues to exceed everyone's expectations for him, whether on the basketball court

# CHAPTER 7

or in the marketing arena," Falk said. "By matching him with some of the cornerstones of American marketing—Nike, McDonald's, Coca-Cola, Wheaties—we've created a real synergy which ties each of the companies together and further enhances his name recognition."

ProServ's deal with Nike actually saved that shoe company from a possible bankruptcy, as more than 60,000 pairs of the Air Jordan gym shoes were purchased in the first three months. Sales have long since gone into the millions with Michael reaping a generous percentage. Jordan is given an endless supply of complimentary shoes, along with sweats, warmups, and other Nike sports apparel. He wears a brand-new pair of shoes for each game, initially breaking them in during shoot-around practices eight hours before tipoff. He gives away his shoes to various charities, the ballboys, or friends after games.

Jordan is very loyal to the products he endorses, realizing in his own way the better they sell, the more money he eventually makes—as if he needs more! He'll walk up to a pop machine and if there isn't any Coca-Colas, he'll scan the choices to see if there are any Coca-Cola by-products. He refuses to drink Pepsi-Cola. It's the same with shoes. He constantly chides anyone wearing a competitive brand. He's probably never been inside a Burger King or Wendy's in his life.

Michael's popularity is at an all-time high, and firms are beside themselves trying to become associated with him. What he represents is a slice of life in the best of America's tradition, the small-town boy who made it big, Horatio Alger discovers jet propulsion. Michael has gone from his self-described "goony-looking" high school portrait to the covers of *GQ, Esquire,* and *Sports Illustrated* magazines. He has made guest appearances on *The Tonight Show* with Johnny Carson, *The David Letterman Show, The Arsenio Hall Show, The Today Show, Good Morning, America,* and was featured on *60 Minutes.* He was offered a part in the movie *Heaven Is A Playground* but backed out when actual filming took more than a year to get arranged.

Jordan's tremendous popularity is not limited to the boundaries of the United States. He has become an equally huge phenomenon overseas, particularly in Europe, where basketball is *the* fast-growing sport. After a recent visit to Holland, American tourists came home wide-eyed with tales of Dutch teenagers wearing all manner of Jordan paraphernalia, imitating his basketball moves right down to hanging their tongues out. A Bulls game on television in the town of Huizen is treated like a national holiday.

In Germany, one American girl stared in disbelief when a young German teenage boy walked past her with his head shaved and only the initials "MJ" standing out. The American girl lived in Germany for three years and experienced the Deutsch version of Jordanmania first hand. "The kids at Vogelweh Air Force Base dressed like him, acted like him, wore his wristbands, kneepads, shoes, and Air Jordan T-shirts," said Joyce Okamoto. "The basketball players on our school team tried to do his dunks. Kids would come to class all red-eyed in the morning after staying up till 4 a.m. to watch a Bulls game. They'd look up his past, where he went to school. They'd cut out all the pictures and articles of him in the newspapers and magazines and put them all over their lockers. Kids would beg and plead for a Michael Jordan poster."

With GM Jerry Krause (left), Michael shows his contract that averages $3 million a year through 1995.

# MIDAS TOUCH

*Sports Illustrated* did a feature on Pennsylvania schoolgirl Michelle Marciniak, touted as the No. 1 high school player in the country who went to Notre Dame to play basketball. Her idol had been former Maryland star Len Bias until he died from cocaine overdose. She was 12 years old at a basketball camp when she heard the news and began to cry. Whenever she played, she used to put a picture of Bias in her sock. Since that day, she has transferred her allegiance to Jordan. Her bedroom has a collection of 30 posters and photos of Jordan covering the walls, and there are 25 pairs of Nikes piled up in her closet. That Bias photo in her sock has been replaced by one of Jordan. "Actually, it's in my sneaker now because I've started wearing short socks," Marciniak told *Sports Illustrated* just before pulling a photo out of her left Nike. "See, I always have him facing outside, toward the court. Michael became my hero after Lenny died. I just admire his ability, his approach to the game." She confided to *Sports Illustrated* that when she goes on road trips, she packs a Jordan "traveling poster" for inspiration.

The love affair kids have with Michael Jordan is a two-way feeling. No. 23 is crazy about kids. Now a father with two boys, Jeffrey Michael and Michael Jeffrey Jr., Jordan once wondered if he could have a kid without being married. That was in his fun-loving, free-wheeling, carefree bachelor days when having a child had more appeal for him than having a wife. His long-time girlfriend, Juanita Vanoy, eventually impressed on him the virtues of family

# CHAPTER 7

life; they were married in 1989 in a secret ceremony in Las Vegas. As it usually does, though, word leaked out and the groom was blitzed with autograph requests instead of being bombarded with rice on his way to the bridal limousine.

The couple first met at a postgame gathering in Bennigan's on Michigan Avenue in Chicago one night after a game during Michael's rookie year. Juanita was a secretary for a downtown firm and wasn't a big pro basketball fan. She had little idea the man she was talking to was the Bulls' franchise. "That's what I liked about her, that she cared about me as a person and not because I played for the Bulls," Jordan said. "People may think this sounds crazy, but it was sometimes hard for me to meet the right girls. You're always wondering if they want to be with you just because you're a pro ballplayer and making a lot of money. How can you be sure they really like you for who you are? I tried to be very careful when I was younger about who I went out with." Jordan had been linked with track athlete Kim Gallagher during the '84 Olympic Games in Los Angeles and briefly saw actress Robin Givens.

Michael's affinity for kids is the real thing. During his rookie season, the Bulls were out of town over Halloween weekend. Before he left, though, Jordan pinned this note to his townhouse door: "Kids: Sorry I missed you for Halloween. If you still want trick-or-treat, come back in three days."

Being a world-famous celebrity isn't always fun and games. An ordinary errand, such as shopping for furniture, becomes a big deal if you're in his Nikes.

# MIDAS TOUCH

What Michael does is call up an exclusive furniture store and make arrangements to visit the store after hours. That way, he can browse and make his selection without having to sign a hundred autographs along the way. The way Jordan spends money, stores are only too happy to oblige. After all, we're talking about the same guy who owns a Porsche, a Mercedes Benz, a Ferrari, a Corvette, a Chevy Blazer, a BMW, and, at one time, also had a personal limousine at his service.

Michael does his formal shopping in Paris, once purchasing 18 tailored business suits. When it comes to meetings with corporate heads and CEOs, Jordan has just the right look. At one time, he would wear business glasses that were nonprescription, plain-glass eyewear, which he said gave him a more intelligent, serious look for his financial gatherings. Jordan prides himself on his business acumen, looking to strike the right image with board members. He keeps tabs on his financial affairs, aware of the disasters like the one that cost Kareem Abdul-Jabbar millions of dollars in bad investments. Jordan's appearance fee for one hour can reach as much as $15,000, and yet he still is forced to turn down requests for lack of time.

Everything he touches turns to gold. His new video, *Michael Jordan's Playground* is already the top-selling sports video in history. His voice will be used in an animated Saturday morning kids' show called *ProStars* that debuts in the fall. He is comfortable in front of the camera and his outgoing personality comes across well. Producers who have

# CHAPTER 7

worked with him on filming commercials and videos marvel at how quickly he adapts to acting techniques and demands. Most claim it is his outgoing nature that allows him to appear so comfortable on camera.

In-between promotional appearances, filming commercials, charity appearances (such as signing autographs for crippled children at the St. Jude's Research Hospital in Memphis), a typical Jordan offseason is filled to the brim with golf events. Jordan was in Memphis for the Federal Express-St. Jude Classic Pro-Am Tournament and took time off to visit kids at the hospital.

"Michael reaches out with his heart to children with special needs," mom Deloris Jordan said. "You know, it really does make him feel good that he can have that effect on kids, and the kids just love him. These sick children look up to Michael so, and I think it gives them some hope to make their wishes come true."

The summer of 1988 was filled with a dozen appearances to participate in various pro-am golf tournaments around the country. Barbara Allen has been Michael's appointments manager, trying to keep pace with one of the world's busiest celebrities. He was a guest on *The Today Show* in New York and later that day accepted the Seagram's Award as the league's top player. He spent time working at his basketball camp in North Carolina and also the one at Illinois Benedictine College in Lisle, a suburb west of Chicago. His Chicago-area camp has since been relocated to Elmhurst College.

Later that year he headed up the first annual

# MIDAS TOUCH

McDonald's Golf Invitational in west suburban Lemont to raise money for the Ronald McDonald House charity. There were 117 celebrities of various kinds who participated in the event along with many top executives from major corporations in Chicago. The outing raised more than $50,000 and included Jordan, sports announcer Brent Musburger, and former Chicago Bears superstar running backs Walter Payton and Gale Sayers. The tournament received front-page coverage and was the highlight of the television news that night.

Other activities that summer included preparing for his role in the movie *Heaven Is A Playground;* leading the annual Bud Billiken Day Parade in Chicago; taking part in the Special Olympics Summer Games at Notre Dame; and coaching Patrick Ewing, James Worthy, and Dominique Wilkins in a three-on-three exhibition game against three winners of a national drawing. Michael finally took time off for a European vacation that included stops in Italy and Monte Carlo.

You may have noticed his affinity for the game of golf. The sport that cannot be completely mastered provides the ultimate challenge for a multitalented athlete with an endless burning desire to compete. What both frustrates and fascinates Jordan is golf's unpredictability and how he can never control the game. He is fond of saying he can make free throws practically anytime he wants. Even those triple-pump, over-the-shoulder, double-reverse, topspin-off-the-glass layups fall in more often than some of Jordan's putts, even though he is a six-

Michael Jordan's picture on a Wheaties box confirms his all-
American image as a role model
for all children.

handicap golfer who has been known to inflate his handicap to 10 or 12 while negotiating side bets. He said that after he retires from the NBA, he wants to join the PGA Seniors Circuit.

It appears that Jordan first got interested in golf while in college, learning the game from a fellow Tar Heel, Davis Love III, now a PGA tour golfer. Michael can drive the ball long distances with accuracy. The part of his game that is his weakest is probably his irons.

Jordan's competitive nature is the stuff of legends. Like all superstars, he hates to lose. At anything. He will pout and carry on if he loses a game of Monopoly. He will persevere and play against superior ping-pong players, refusing to stop playing until he wins a game or two. In card games, he is a zealous player. He shot pool as a rookie and had a difficult time beating close friend Rod Higgins (now with Golden State). Jordan got so frustrated that he bought a pool table and practiced on it every day. Finally, he got to be Higgins's equal, and then some. The only Bull he couldn't beat consistently was Quintin Dailey, who learned the game growing up on the mean streets of South Baltimore and eventually went on to become a two-time Maryland state champion pool shooter. Michael's hand-eye coordination was so good that after testing out very high at a pistol range, he was offered an opportunity to enroll in the police academy to begin training as a SWAT squad marksman.

During the Bulls' training camp at Beloit (Wisconsin) College in 1986, the team had taken a

# CHAPTER 7

day off for a golf outing with corporate sponsors and the media. After the steak dinner, Jordan began hustling on the pool table, taking on all comers at $5 a game. One by one the challengers would succumb, as Jordan's hand would be out with his tongue wagging happily. He was laughing and talking and sinking shots, psyching out opponents with his chatter.

At one point, a 10-year-old boy who was very good took Michael on and it came down to the final ball, which Jordan sunk. The little boy put his head down when Jordan asked him for the $5. The kid obviously thought Jordan would never make him pay. He dug deep into his pocket, pulled it out, looked at it, and handed it over. Jordan gave him a serious look and reminded the boy that if he was going to gamble in life, he'd better be ready to pay the price if he lost.

Next came Jordan's biggest challenge. Up stepped the local pool shark, to the applause of those watching. There was a buzz in the audience of 75 or so onlookers, whispers that the cocky star would finally meet his match. Jordan sized up his opponent, studying how he screwed together his custom-made pool cue and made note of his mannerisms. This was fourth-quarter crunch time, Georgetown against North Carolina, Magic against Michael. His mood turned swiftly from fun-loving to somber and the smile was put on layaway. He stood silently watching his opponent warm up and noticing how softly he shot.

They went at each other in a classic battle right

out of the Paul Newman and Jackie Gleason movie, *The Hustler*. Michael looked concerned, but his competitive juices were flowing. It seems that the bigger the challenge you put before him, the higher he will rise to the occasion. It came down to a difficult shot. If Jordan made it, he won. If not, the local shark would be home free.

There was a look of total concentration on Jordan's face as he lined up the shot. It was the same kind of intensity he had displayed six months earlier when he had hit two free throws with time expired to force a second overtime in the 135-131 playoff loss to the Celtics. Finally, Jordan took a deep breath and let the cue stick glide through his long fingers. Stick met cue ball just right, sending the winning shot on its way to the corner pocket.

Jordan triumphantly pumped his right fist into the air three times, a scene he would re-enact three years later after hitting a last-second shot to eliminate Cleveland from the playoffs. All the locals marveled at how this basketball player had beaten their best. This time, Jordan was a gracious winner, complimenting his opponent and saying how fortunate he had been. When the subject of a rematch was broached, Jordan begged off, saying he had shot too much already. Jordan realized he had beaten a superior opponent and there was no sense pushing his luck.

The 10-year-old kid? Jordan had him rack the balls for that final game and gave him $5 for the chore. The kid walked away with the biggest smile, as if faith in his hero had been restored.

# CHAPTER 8

# Champion

*Left:* Despite having to defend Magic Johnson (right) in the finals, Michael was an offensive force. In the 1991 five-game NBA Finals series against the Lakers, Jordan averaged 31.2 points, 11.4 assists, 6.6 rebounds, and 2.8 steals per game. "It's the most proud day I've ever had," he said.

# CHAPTER 8

MICHAEL JORDAN FINALLY realized his
life-long dream on June 12, 1991. The Bulls
beat the Lakers 108-101 in game five of the
NBA Finals to win the Championship 4-1.

With the Championship series, the NBA finally
got what it wanted. The National Basketball
Association reached then maintained a ten-year
explosion in the 1980s because of a couple of stars,
Larry Bird and Magic Johnson. More than any other
major team sport, pro basketball lends itself to a few
overwhelmingly bright stars. When the Larry and
Magic rivalry waned late in the decade, the powers
that be wanted a fresh new face to encounter the
Lakers' and Magic's showtime: Michael Jordan.
After the 1990-91 season, they got their wish. The
win in a sense vindicated Jordan, who still, even
after elevating his team to new heights, was tagged
with the faulty opinion about how he couldn't make
his teammates better. Advocates who said that Bird
and Magic were better players always pointed to
their rings for validation. Now, Michael was not
only in their club, he was on the board of directors.

Michael, raising his level of play, and that of his
teammates, to Championship caliber, was many years
in the making. The 1988-89 and 1989-90 seasons,
though, were frustrating for Michael, the Bulls as a
team, and the city of Chicago. The Bulls came so
close to the Finals both seasons. And the despised
Detroit Pistons came away with the trophies both
years. In October 1988, the Bulls weren't considered
one of the top five teams in the circuit. It took a
miraculous Jordan jumper to propel them to that

level. Few basketball players get the opportunity to hit a dramatic, game-winning shot that has so much impact it will go down in history, yet Michael has been twice-blessed. First came the game-winner that gave North Carolina the NCAA championship over Georgetown in 1982. Then, seven years later, after the 1988-89 season, Jordan hit a difficult shot that began the deterioration of a one-time NBA title contender.

The tape of his last-second shot that eliminated the Cleveland Cavaliers from the 1989 playoffs has been replayed countless times. With six seconds left in the game and Cleveland trailing by a point, Cavs coach Lenny Wilkens unveiled a piece of brilliant strategy. He had Craig Ehlo inbounds the ball. No Bulls paid much attention to Ehlo—with stars Mark Price, Larry Nance, and Ron Harper the likely big-shot choices—Craig snuck past the Bulls defense, took a return pass, and scored a layup virtually unmolested.

This was the final game in a bitterly contested best-of-five first-round Eastern Conference playoff series. It was the second year in a row the two Central Division adversaries had met, with the Cavs having the better team on paper both times. The year before, they lost game five in Chicago as Jordan averaged a record-breaking 45.2 points a game. That after Cleveland had battled Detroit all season for the division title. The Cavs were being called the NBA's team of the 1990s.

There were three seconds left when the Bulls inbounded the ball from halfcourt with 20,000

# CHAPTER 8

Cavaliers fans in Richfield Coliseum screaming for the home team to hold on for just three ticks of the clock. Everybody in the building and indeed, across America watching this national telecast, knew where the ball was going. Bulls' assistant coach John Bach had long ago nicknamed this the "Archangel Offense." Said Bach: "That's where we put the ball in his hands and say, 'Save us, Michael.'"

Jordan broke to the ball with Nance and Ehlo in hot pursuit. Ehlo was Jordan's defender and Nance simply abandoned his assignment, so intent was he on stopping Jordan. Michael got the ball, pivoted, took a dribble past Nance, and from the right of the free-throw line took off. Jordan pumped once as his body drifted horizontally to the left, freeing himself from Ehlo, who appeared to give Jordan a little nudge. Still gliding to his left, Jordan shot the ball at the basket. It was the same sensation as hitting a moving target. Somehow, Jordan swished the 15-footer for a 101-100 victory. He landed on both feet, leaped into the air, and waved his fist once. Michael was mobbed by his ecstatic teammates. The Richfield Coliseum turned into a gigantic mausoleum as 20,000 stunned partisans sat in silence not wanting to believe what they had just witnessed.

"There's nothing like it in the world, that feeling of having the ball in the final seconds as the clock slowly ticks off, going up and hanging in the air and then hitting the shot," Jordan said. "Man, that is total control. There's just no other feeling like it, none."

The repercussions of that shot are still being felt

# CHAMPION

by the Cavaliers today. Frustrated—and upset at being eliminated in the first round by a Bulls team they considered inferior to them—Cavs management made some drastic changes. Harper was dealt to the L.A. Clippers for Danny Ferry, several of the Cavs younger players were traded away, and the focus of the team changed. The Cavaliers haven't been NBA contenders since while the Bulls have gone on to challenge the Pistons for Eastern Conference supremacy twice. In the 1990-91 season, Chicago was the NBA Champion. If not for that shot, both teams' fortunes could easily be reversed today.

In the 1989 playoffs, the Bulls went on to defeat the New York Knicks 4-2. Despite pulling a groin muscle, Jordan averaged 35.6 points and 9.6 rebounds in the six games. In the opener, he registered his first playoff triple-double with 34 points, 12 assists, and 10 rebounds.

The Bulls again fell short against the Pistons, losing in six games. For the postseason, Jordan averaged 34.8 points, eight assists, and seven rebounds as he began demonstrating to critics he was more than simply a scorer. He did replace Bob Love as the club's all-time leading playoffs scorer.

Coming off the high of their 50-win season of 1987-88, the Bulls fell off a bit the following year, finishing 47-35, fifth-best in the Eastern Conference. Jordan won his third-straight league scoring title, averaging 32.5 points a game. He was third in the NBA in steals and 10th in assists. He was awarded the Schick Pivotal Player of the Year honor and also the *The Sporting News* named him Player of the

# CHAPTER 8

Year. He scored 52 points three times in November, burning the Celtics, 76ers, and Nuggets. In Denver, he broke his own club record by scoring 30 points in the fourth quarter. He had an NBA and season-high 53 points in a loss to Phoenix in January and four days later scored 33 points against the 76ers to reach the 10,000-point milestone faster than any other player except Wilt Chamberlain. Switched to point guard in a coach Doug Collins experiment, Jordan had a stretch where he recorded seven consecutive triple-doubles, the best of any player in the league. He finished the season with 15 triple-doubles, including 12 in the final 24 games.

Bulls TV analyst Johnny "Red" Kerr has been an NBA player, coach, and is now a broadcaster, and he has seen it all. He claims Jordan is the best. "Michael is the greatest competitor I've ever seen," Kerr told Knight-Ridder's Ray Didinger. "[Jordan] has great talent, but the thing that makes him exceptional is he comes to play every night. Most guys will take one game off now and then. Not Michael Jordan. He plays every game to the hilt. I've been around a lot of megatalented players. I signed Julius Erving to his first ABA contract in Virginia. I had George Gervin there, too. They were damn good, but they weren't like this kid. Where Julius was smooth going to the basket, like poetry, Michael is vicious. He attacks you. I honestly believe this kid is the best player who ever walked on a court. He does more things than anybody."

Collins coached Jordan for three years before being fired by the Bulls and winding up as a TV

analyst with cable station TNT. "There is nothing
Michael can't do," Collins told Didinger. "I love
Dennis Rodman (Pistons), but Michael plays tougher
defense than Dennis. If you polled the NBA guards
and asked them to pick the one man they'd least like
to have guard them in the last 24 seconds of a game,
I'll bet most of them would pick Michael. And, if
you asked them to pick the one player they would
least like to defend in the last 24 seconds, it would
be Michael by a landslide. That's a pretty nice
compliment. In crunch time, this one guy is the best
at both ends of the floor. I don't know if there's
ever been another player like that."

Jordan reached another milestone during the 1989-
90 season when he torched Cleveland for a career-
high 69 points in a 117-113 overtime win at the
Richfield Coliseum in March. Think the folks
around there aren't just a little bit tired of seeing
Jordan fly in the face of their heroes? Jordan also
had a career-high 18 rebounds in that game along
with six assists and four steals. Figuring the six
assists led to 12 points, Jordan was directly
accountable for 81 of the 117 points the Bulls
scored. Only three players in NBA history—
Chamberlain, David Thompson, and Elgin Baylor—
have ever scored more in a game. Afterward,
whether he was just being a sore loser and getting
frustrated at the treatment Jordan has accorded him,
Cavs coach Lenny Wilkens ripped No. 23 for taking
too many shots. Jordan would later respond that
perhaps it was Wilkens's defensive scheme that left
him open for so many easy shots. The Cavs' John

# CHAPTER 8

Williams called Jordan "one in a billion" afterwards.

"It was one of those nights where everything went right," Jordan told Didinger. "I got on a roll early and found myself in a great rhythm. I kept pushing myself, talking to myself, saying, 'Don't stop. Keep going.' It was definitely fun."

The 1989-90 season was Michael's sixth season, and his fifth full season discounting his sophomore year because he missed 64 games with a broken foot. He supplanted Love as the Bulls' all-time leading scorer, as Jordan won his fourth consecutive scoring title, averaging 33.6 points a game. He also led the NBA in steals with 2.77 a game. Expanding his game, he also averaged 6.9 rebounds and 6.3 assists a game while leading the Bulls to a 55-27 record, their best in 18 years. They wound up with the second-best record in the East, behind only arch-rival Detroit.

There appeared to be no limit to his status as a celebrity. New coach Phil Jackson began to realize this as he attempted to monitor Jordan's off-court distractions. "We try to control the hustle and bustle as best we can, but it's not easy," Jackson told Knight-Ridder. At home, his new policy restricted locker room guests. "There are people trying to get in to see Michael everywhere we go. One night it's Jesse Jackson, the next night it's Spike Lee. We go to L.A. and it's Timothy Hutton and Brooke Shields." Jackson neglected to mention others who have sought Jordan out, including Hollywood stars Charlie Sheen, Billy Crystal, and Gregory Hines. Singer Whitney Houston, quarterback Boomer

# CHAMPION

Esiason, golfer Raymond Floyd, and tennis star John McEnroe are among others. Also, there's always Michael's work with the Michael Jordan Foundation he established that is managed by Anne Armstrong. It's his own personal charity where he tries to help unfortunate kids as much as possible.

"Every city we visit, I get calls from parents with handicapped kids or terminally ill kids whose only wish is to meet Michael Jordan," Bulls media relations director Tim Hallam told Ray Didinger. "The parents say: 'It will only take 10 minutes and it will mean so much.' But they don't realize we have practices and meetings on the road. Maybe Michael has an injury and needs treatment. It's not easy. But I'll ask Michael, and it's incredible what he agrees to do. The last time we were in Washington, D.C., he saw five kids. People ask if he ever loses his temper. I can honestly say I've never seen his happen, not once in the seven years I've worked with him. There are times when he will draw the line. If it's a big game, he will say to me: 'Tonight, I'm playing ball.' That means he doesn't want to do interviews or shake hands before the game, he wants to concentrate. But most of the time he's very easy, very accessible."

There was a time just after another game in Washington where Jordan had a rough night in a loss to the Bullets and couldn't fall asleep until almost 2 a.m. He was up at 6:30 a.m. and off to George Washington gym for a special appearance. *USA Today's* Tom Weir accompanied Michael to a workout with kids involved in the Special Olympics,

# CHAPTER 8

Michael passes off around Patrick Ewing to a teammate.
The Championship proved that Jordan could elevate his
team to new heights.

most of them suffering from a congenital disease known as Down's syndrome, which often claims the life of its victims before the age of 40. Weir reported that one of them, Freddy Lockett, walked up to Jordan and said: "I've seen you on TV. You ain't that tough." To which Jordan responded: "You and me, Freddy, one-on-one."

"I don't really get sad looking at them," Jordan told Weir. "There's always good with the bad. I'm sad you have situations like this, of course. You know, why can't everybody be like myself? But some of these kids are really competitive. They want to play and they want to learn. I feel I do owe something. With all that I've achieved, this is the least I can do."

Just before he left, Jordan performed a couple of sky-dunks that wowed his admirers. Tough little Freddy tried guarding Jordan on one of his moves. "Took you to the hoop," Jordan said with a smile. "But we'll met up again." As Jordan got up to leave, a little girl named Tania bowed her head and began to cry. Jordan got her attention, told her to look up at him and gave her a big hug.

The Bulls knocked off the Bucks 3-1 in the first round of the 1989-90 playoffs. Chicago then got by the troublesome 76ers 4-1, with Jordan scoring 49 points in game three at the Spectrum. Once again, it was the Motor City against the Second City in the Eastern Conference finals. This time, each team won its home games, with the Pistons squeaking by in the seven-game series with the final game at the Silverdome. This series did mark the first time

# CHAPTER 8

Michael had beaten Detroit's anti-Jordan defense
system when he tallied 47 points in game three and
42 in game four, both wins at the Stadium.

The Bulls had the greatest regular-season success
in franchise history during 1990-91, winning 61
games, the most in the Eastern Conference. Michael
won his fifth consecutive scoring crown with 31.5
points per game. He also averaged six rebounds and
five and one-half assists per game, and totaled 223
steals. These numbers would be astounding for any
other player in the league. By his seventh season,
though, these stats seem almost mundane for
Michael Jordan.

"I just try to have the best season possible and be
as consistent as possible," Michael said. "This year
is a little more special because my teammates have
really stepped up to give me the contribution I have
needed and we have needed to put us in a position
to win" the NBA Finals. "My stats have been very
similar in the last few years, but the team's success
in winning 61 games has enabled me to win the
MVP Award."

The Bulls won the top spot in the Eastern
Conference playoffs and faced the eighth-seeded
New York Knicks, who had been slipping into a
second-rank team for several seasons. Michael and
the Bulls showed the New Yorkers that they meant
business from the opening tip. After Chicago won
the first game of the playoffs 126-85, Knicks all-
world center Patrick Ewing said, "I'm frustrated by
the whole situation. They whipped us, beat us by
41." The Bulls won the final two games of the series

as well, then went to the Stadium to await Sir
Charles Barkley and the unruly 76ers.

The Sixers roared into Chicago Stadium after
beating up on the Milwaukee Bucks, but the Bulls
beat Philadelphia 105-92 to give Barkley & Co. a
hard way to go. After the Bulls won game two 112-
100 the series moved to Philly for game three.
Hersey Hawkins popped a three with seconds left to
give a Chicago opponent the first victory in the
playoffs. The Bulls then beat the Sixers 101-85 and
100-95, with Michael averaging 33.4 points during
the five games. "I thought we had a good shot,"
Philadelphia coach Jim Lynam said after the series
was finished, "but Jordan took over."

When the Pistons rolled into town, the entire city
of Chicago could see only red. Especially Michael.
Jordan got into the face of the Pistons, of Joe
Dumars and Dennis Rodman, proving to the Motor
City mad men that the Bulls would not be
intimidated.

What the Bulls did was terrify Detroit with their
defense, their quickness, and their ability to explode
offensively. Michael did not have a good game one,
shooting six-for-15 for 22 points and turning the ball
over six times, yet the Bulls won 94-83. "I didn't
shoot the ball well today, and I basically had a bad
game, at least offensively," Michael said. "You've
got to give my supporting cast a lot of credit. We
proved we're a well-balanced team and that other
guys can come in and step up." Jordan stepped up
his game, scoring 35 points in game two, a 105-97
win at Chicago Stadium; scoring 33 points in game

# CHAPTER 8

three, a 113-97 win in Detroit; and scoring 29 in a
115-94 win to sweep the defending World Champs
on their home turf.

The Lakers "Showtime" offense of the 1980s had
been transformed into a post-up "Slowtime" offense
similar to that of the Boston Celtics in 1990-91.
With Magic, James Worthy, Sam Perkins, and Vlade
Divac, Los Angeles still had the horses to romp
through the Western Conference and upset the
favored Portland Trail Blazers. The Bulls were now
the team that played with a run-and-gun philosophy
with which the Lakers had used to win many
championships.

The Lakers looked like the grizzled champions in
the first game of the series, winning at the Chicago
Stadium 93-91. Sam Perkins, Michael's old college
teammate at North Carolina, fired a three-point shot
to provide the winning margin. Jordan could not
match the shot seconds later, when he missed on an
18-footer. The Bulls looked in disarray after game
one, but Michael, was the picture of calm. The
series' two foes, Magic and Michael, didn't
disappoint. Magic had a triple-double, and Jordan
scored 36 points with 12 rebounds and eight assists,
"It was a great game," he said, "and it took a North
Carolina guy to beat me. We played good enough to
win. Whoever made the plays down the stretch was
going to win. We had the opportunity and they had
the opportunity. Ours just rattled out."

The Bulls came back to rout L.A. in game two
107-86. "We were very nervous in the first game,"
Michael (who scored 33 points) said. "I knew we'd

be more relaxed tonight. We didn't do things differently, it was just that our energy level was higher." Scottie Pippen scored 20 points, but more important took over much of the defensive burden of guarding Magic and did a masterful job. On the other hand, Michael again proved his versatility by moving to low post defense to guard Vlade Divac. Horace Grant (20 points), Bill Cartwright (12), and John Paxson (16) contributed on the offensive end.

Regaining the momentum, Michael and the Bulls flew into Los Angeles looking to take it to the purple and yellow at the Great Western Forum. The Lakers switched gears and pounded the ball down low to Perkins (25 points), Divac (24), and Worthy (19). Magic also provided 22 points. Chicago, however, rolled back from a 13-point third quarter deficit to tie the game at 92 on a clutch Jordan jumper. Michael then unleashed six points in O.T. to R.I.P L.A. 104-96.

Their backs to the wall, the Lakers were prepared to blast the Bulls in game four. It was Chicago, however, that lacquered L.A. with a suffocating defense, winning 97-82. Michael had 28 points and a career playoff best 13 assists. Magic scored 22 points and had 11 assists, and Divac had 27 points and 11 rebounds. The numbers tell the rest of Chicago's defensive story: Perkins one-for-15 for three points; Worthy six-for-16 for 12 points; Scott four points; Terry Teagle one-for-six for six points; A.C. Green one-for-five for five points. "We've got a great opportunity to finish it now," Michael said. "But, we know it's not going to be easy."

# CHAPTER 8

Jordan is a better player than prognosticator. While the Lakers gave it a good try, the 108-101 clincher was not, in reality, much in doubt. Magic scored 16 with 20 assists and 11 rebounds, and Elden Campbell came off the bench to score 21. But Paxson hit 10 points at the end of the fourth quarter to guarantee the series.

"It means so much," Jordan said after the Championship victory. "All the things I've gone through, all the things the city has gone through. It was a lot of hard work, and what you see is the emotions of all that hard work paying off. Not just for me but for this team and this city. It was a seven-year struggle. It's the most proud day I've ever had." Michael had 30 points and 10 assists in game five, to finish the series averaging 31.2 points, 11.4 assists, 6.6 rebounds, and 2.8 steals per game. He said this about being named Finals MVP: "I could care less. The whole team is the MVP. The whole city is the MVP."

Even though he received the ring, Michael won't forget a tragedy that took place that season. For six years, he had entered into a close friendship with Mickey Gitlitz, the personable, fun-loving owner of the Multiplex Fitness Club in north suburban Deerfield, where the Bulls practice. Gitlitz had practically become a father figure to Michael, and he often confided his biggest concerns and even problems of a personal nature to Gitlitz. Jordan felt secure in the confidentiality of their relationship, and Gitlitz guarded closely all secrets that Jordan revealed to him.

# CHAMPION

They were great golfing buddies, often playing with Gitlitz's son Scott, and never for free. There were dozens of side bets established as money went back and forth quicker than at a stock exchange. Jordan's constant chattering and other distractive ploys didn't always work. Mickey was a top-notch golfer and always in peak condition for a man in his early 50s. Scott, in his late 20s, was good enough to play on his college golf team at the University of South Florida, where a couple of his former teammates are now on the PGA Tour.

Once, on a plane returning from a vacation in Italy, Jordan phoned Gitlitz and asked him to set up a tee time for when he landed. Mickey and Scott were frequent guests at Jordan's home, but always careful not to let the friendship infringe on Jordan. Michael really appreciated that and looked upon them as friends he could trust. Once, while establishing stakes for another round, Jordan asked Gitlitz if they could up the ante.

"What would you like to play for," Mickey said with a smile. "How about your club?" Jordan responded with a serious look. Gitlitz was taken aback and momentarily speechless until Jordan let loose with a howl.

It was in November 1990 that Gitlitz died from a cancerous brain tumor that he had battled for nearly two years. It was a courageous fight, inspiring all those who came in contact with him. During that time, whenever Jordan had problems, when maybe the jumper wasn't falling or other aspects of his life weren't to his liking, he would remember his dear

# CHAPTER 8

friend Mickey and put everything in the right perspective. His friend's death left him at a loss.

It was a painful reminder that as much as Michael Jordan would love for the world to be fun and games and carefree times, a place where laughter and joy are the music we dance to, it can't always be. Even if you are Michael Jordan, a multimillionaire capable of doing almost anything, there are things you cannot control. Deloris once said her famous son hates to see anyone suffering, hates to see anything bad happen. She recalls the incident where one of Michael's good friends in college drowned. He felt helpless, and only wanted to make things right. There is a tremendous amount of good he can do. He knows this. Yet, there are times when he wants to do more, and can't.

As much as anything, he wishes he had the power to heal Mickey Gitlitz. He wishes he could magically cure the tragic illnesses of terminally ill children. He wants everyone in the world to smile more than they frown, to rejoice more than they hurt. This is the compassionate, human side of Michael Jordan, a young man who remains as caring and considerate today as he was back in Wilmington, North Carolina.

Another issue that tore at his heart was the wave of attacks and killings over his Air Jordan shoes. The Nike product had reached such a revered status in the underprivileged areas of inner cities that teenage gang members were holding up kids and in some cases shooting them over a pair of shoes. Jordan felt terrible about the incidents and there was talk he might even suspend endorsement until things cooled down.

"I don't think it's a Michael Jordan problem or a Nike problem," he told Knight-Ridder. "I think it's a society problem. Kids are committing crimes for all kinds of reasons. There's another side to this. I've heard from parents who say: 'My son got a job so he could earn the money to buy a pair of your shoes.' They like the fact that it gives kids something to work toward. That's a healthy thing. But when kids steal and hurt each other, that's bad.

"I don't know what to do about it. If we stop making the shoes, will crime go away? All this time, you reporters held me up as a good role model. Now, I'm being portrayed as a murderer by some writers. It bothers me a lot. I know what Michael Jordan stands for, and hurting people isn't it. I think most people understand that. At least I hope they do, because it's the truth."

None of us, not even Michael Jordan, can make time stand still. It's as if Peter Pan has grown up. Even so, Jordan will always have fun. He was once asked to describe himself.

"He's a fun-loving person, he smiles, he's outgoing and he tries to do the best he can at whatever he does. He feels like he's a role model for kids, and I would say he's good-looking." With that Jordan let loose a grin, "but that might be saying too much."

# CHAPTER 8

## STATS

### Regular Season

|        | G   | Reb Avg | Asst Avg | Pts Avg |
|--------|-----|---------|----------|---------|
| 84-85  | 82  | 6.5     | 5.9      | 28.2    |
| 85-86  | 18  | 3.6     | 2.9      | 22.7    |
| 86-87  | 82  | 5.2     | 4.6      | 37.1    |
| 87-88  | 82  | 5.5     | 5.9      | 35.0    |
| 88-89  | 81  | 8.0     | 8.0      | 32.5    |
| 89-90  | 82  | 6.9     | 6.3      | 33.6    |
| 90-91  | 82  | 6.0     | 5.5      | 31.5    |
| Totals | 509 | 6.3     | 5.9      | 32.7    |

### Playoffs

|        | G  | Reb Avg | Asst Avg | Pts Avg |
|--------|----|---------|----------|---------|
| 84-85  | 4  | 5.8     | 8.5      | 29.3    |
| 85-86  | 3  | 6.3     | 5.7      | 43.7    |
| 86-87  | 3  | 7.0     | 6.0      | 35.7    |
| 87-88  | 10 | 7.1     | 4.7      | 36.3    |
| 88-89  | 17 | 7.0     | 7.7      | 34.8    |
| 89-90  | 16 | 7.2     | 6.8      | 36.7    |
| 90-91  | 17 | 6.4     | 8.4      | 31.1    |
| Totals | 70 | 6.8     | 7.1      | 34.6    |